MEDIÆVAL HYMNS

THE

HYMN OF HILDEBERT

AND OTHER

MEDIÆVAL HYMNS

WITH TRANSLATIONS

BY ERASTUS C. BENEDICT

A NEW AND ENLARGED EDITION

NEW YORK
ANSON D. F. RANDOLPH & CO.
1868

Bradstreet Press.

PREFACE.

THESE translations have been the agreeable labor of occasional hours of leisure. Several of them have at different times, during the last fifteen years, appeared in public journals, literary and religious, and the favorable mention made of some of them has induced me to collect those which have been published, and to add some others, including the Hymn of Hildebert to the Trinity. Of some of them, previous translations are numerous and excellent.

In making this selection, my aim has been to bring together such a variety of hymns and topics as should, in small compass, exhibit the evangelical faith and character of those eminent and devout men, whose light shone so purely in that period of Christianity which we call the Middle Ages; their ideas of God and his attributes, of the Father, the Son, and the Holy Spirit; their knowledge of the Scriptures; their exhaustive treatment of their topics, and their modes of thought and expression, so simple and unpretentious. I was also especially influenced by a desire to exhibit that oneness of evangelical faith, and that Christian union in the great characteristic and essential elements of our holy religion, which enables us to acknowledge our brotherhood with these simple-minded, cultivated, and sanctified men, who devoted their lives to religion as it was presented by the Saviour and his sacred family, and their early successors, appealing to the heart instead of to the senses, and manifesting itself in great but simple and intelligible truths, and not in forms and rites, and ceremonies and vestments. I make little account of the fact that they may have believed something which I cannot believe, and may have used a ritual and liturgy which I disapprove. I never stop to think that the authors of the "Imitation of Christ," of the "Holy Living and Dying," of the "Pilgrim's Progress," held to points of faith, and used rites and modes of worship different from mine, any more than I do that the holy apostles themselves, who were with the Lord continually, and listened to those daily teachings which drew such crowds of hearers, and who saw all his miracles, were, even after the resurrection, still ignorant of the nature of his kingdom, of his sacrifice, and of his great salvation.

I make no apology for the simplicity and naturalness of these translations. It would have been less laborious and difficult, to make translations which, to certain tastes, would have been more agreeable, and would have seemed more poetical—expanded paraphrases—English hymns founded upon the Latin ones, intensified by epithets and ornamented with imagery. My own taste, however, found a great charm in the great simplicity and brevity of the originals, and I preferred to translate those striking qualities. I have accordingly kept the English version within the length of the Latin original, and have endeavored to perform this task, certainly difficult, and sometimes said to be impossible, without sacrificing ease in versification, or the meaning and spirit of the original. How far I have succeeded must be left to the judgment of others.

In most cases also I have adopted the stanza and measure of the original, and the double rhymes and dactylic terminations so common with those Latin hymnologists. I do not share the opinion sometimes expressed, that in our language such rhymes are inconsistent with the dignity, gravity, and tenderness which may be expressed by them in Latin, and without which sacred hymns would lose their character. To this opinion, perhaps, may be attributed the fact, that in the English version of the psalms by Dr. Watts, there are no double rhymes, except three couplets in his translation of the Fiftieth Psalm, and in the versions of Tate and Brady, and of Sternhold and Hopkins none, and that the earlier translations of the *Dies Iræ* were made in single rhyme. Many of the more recent ones, however, are made with double rhyme, and I apprehend that the opinion is now general that the true spirit and solemnity of that great hymn are better exhibited in some of the double rhyme translations than they are in any others. When the line is trochaic, the trochaic ending preserves, instead of impairing, the tone and feeling of the lines—which may be expressive of any sentiment, however grave or tender. Many of the sweetest and most devotional hymns in our language, are in double rhyme, and I need refer only to the grace and dignity, as well as tenderness and strength, with which Wesley and Heber and others, use the double rhyme, to show the truth of these remarks. I am, indeed, by no means certain that the double rhyme may not in the end, prove to be the higher and better style of versification and rhythm. I incline to the belief that there is in it a more graceful cadence, a more flowing and easy transition, and a more unbroken harmony, than in the sometimes crisp and sharp ending of the single rhyme.

It is surprising that Milton, who used rhyme with admirable skill, should speak of it as the invention of a barbarous age, to set off wretched matter and lame metre. In the universality of rhyme, as in the further fact that it is peculiar neither to the rudeness of an early and barbarous age, nor to the over-refined ingenuity of a late and artificial one, but runs through whole literatures, we find its best defence, and the evidence that it lies deep in our human nature, since otherwise so many peoples would not have lighted upon it, or so inflexibly maintained it; for no people has ever adopted an accentual rhythm without also adopting rhyme, which only in weak and indistinct beginnings makes its first appearance, and with advancing refinement, poetical cultivation, and perfection of language, rises to its highest excellence. It has been well said, that rhyme, well managed, is one of the most pleasing of all inventions for entertaining the mind—constantly raising expectation, and as often satisfying it. The ear anticipates the sound without knowing what the sound would express. This expectation and its gratification are a constant pleasure, different from that conveyed by the thought, but always playing about it, and in harmony with it—like music, adorning and intensifying it. It is hardly to be believed that the classical versification could be native or vernacular to any people, and it is not more easy to believe, that if it had been natural to the Romans, it would have so easily retired before that rhythmical versification which supplanted it. It is worthy of remark, in this connection, that all those peoples, which in our day are spoken of as the Latin race, to distinguish them from the Gothic and Sclavic races, have their poetical literature characterized by rhythmical and accentual versification and by rhyme, and that the metres of Virgil and Horace and Catullus have given place to rhyme and accent, even in the Italian peninsula.

Of some of these hymns (some, indeed, which have been better translated by others) I have made more than one translation. Without assigning any satisfactory reason why I should thus be willing to come into comparison with others of established reputation, I may say that the reason which would induce me to make one translation might well induce me to make several—different tastes being gratified by various forms of presenting the same thoughts. As to the translations of the *Dies Iræ*, I will also say that the second in order was published many years ago, before the thought of using English double rhyme for so serious a purpose, had entered my mind. The third was afterwards written in double rhyme, and, finally, the other was the result of an attempt to use nothing but the Gothic-English language, discarding entirely the use of Latin derivatives. This one being more agreeable to my taste, I have given it the first place.

All these early Latin hymns were written before the invention of printing, and copies were often taken down from memory or learned from oral tradition, which, doubtless, furnishes the reason why, sometimes, one or more stanzas are omitted in some copies, and why the arrangement of the stanzas differs, in different copies of the same hymn. I have followed what seemed to me the best authority for the text, and I have not hesitated to adopt the arrangement of the stanzas which seemed to me the most forcible and beautiful. In like manner I have also substituted a word and changed the arrangement of words in a line, where the rhythm so plainly demanded it as to compel the belief that such was the author's arrangement.

I have preceded most of the hymns with a brief sketch of the supposed author, or a sort of argument of the hymn, or brief commentary upon it. I am, however, far from believing that the authorship of them is thus attributed on sufficient evidence in all cases. There is hardly one that has not been attributed, with equal confidence, to more than one author, and there are few of them whose authorship can be considered as settled, on evidence.

A word more as to the thread by which these hymns are here connected—so slight that, perhaps, it might not be perceived, unless it were pointed out. The Christian faith, life, and hope, founded upon the being and attributes of God; the birth, teachings, sufferings, death, resurrection, ascension, and commemoration of our Lord, and the gift of the Holy Spirit, are exhibited in the order which I have adopted, while the doctrines of faith and grace, and the spirit of devotion, animate the whole.

The careful and learned remarks of the Rev. Dr. Williams in his "Miscellanies," p. 72, of Dr. Coles in his "Dies Iræ," of Dr. Schaff in his "New Stabat Mater," of Dr. Neale in his "Mediæval Hymns," and, above all, the Preface, Introduction, and notes of Archbishop Trench in his "Sacred Latin Poetry," are worthy of careful study by all who desire to be informed on the subject of Latin hymnology. I have read them with the greatest interest, and have borrowed much from them, as well in this preface as elsewhere, for which I desire to make this acknowledgment, because I have almost always neglected to do so in the text of my remarks.

TABLE OF HYMNS.

INDEX.

HILDEBERT.

Hildebert de Lavardin was a Frenchman. He was born in 1057 and was educated in the highest scholarship and culture of his time, having studied under Beranger and St. Hugh of Cluny whose life he wrote. He was consecrated Bishop of Mans in 1097, and in 1125 became Archbishop of Tours and was one of the great ornaments of the French Roman Catholic Church. All the authors of that period speak in his praise. It was commonly said of him,

> Inclytus et prosâ versuque per omnia primus,
> Hildebertus olet prorsus ubique rosam.

His Hymn to the Trinity is every way worthy of him. It is characterized, equally, by harmony and grace and by sententious brevity. Its fullness and discrimination as a theological essay and its easy and familiar use of Scriptural allusion, are quite as remarkable as its gentle spirit of devotion and its poetical animation, in which it has been said to equal the very best productions which Latin Christian poetry can anywhere boast.

The Poem has a sort of epic completeness; its Beginning—the knowledge of God—*Fides orthodoxa*—the true creed, as to the Three Persons of the Holy Trinity—exhibiting their attributes, as the foundation of the Christian character; its Middle—the weakness, the trials and the temptations of the Christian life, in its progress to perfect trust and confidence in God and assurance of His final grace; its End—the joys and glories of the Heavenly Home of the blessed.

HILDEBERTI HYMNUS.

ORATIO DEVOTISSIMA

AD TRES PERSONAS SANCTISSIMÆ TRINITATIS.

AD PATREM.

Alpha et Ω, magne Deus!
Eli! Eli! Deus meus,—
Cujus virtus, totum posse;
Cujus sensus, totum nosse;
Cujus esse, summum bonum;
Cujus opus, quicquid bonum.
Super cuncta, subter cuncta;
Extra cuncta, intra cuncta.
Intra cuncta, nec inclusus;
Extra cuncta, nec exclusus;
Super cuncta, nec elatus;
Subter cuncta, nec substratus.
Super totus, præsidendo;
Subter totus, sustinendo;
Extra totus, complectendo;
Intra totus es, implendo.
Intra, nunquam coarctaris;

HYMN OF HILDEBERT.

AN ADDRESS TO THE THREE PERSONS OF THE MOST HOLY TRINITY.

TO THE FATHER.

Father, God, my God, all seeing!
Alpha and Omega being—
Thou whose power no limit showeth
Thou whose wisdom all things knoweth,
God all good beyond comparing—
God of love for mortals caring—
Over, under, all abounding,
In and out and all surrounding—
Inside all, yet not included,
Outside all, yet not excluded,
Over all, yet not elated,
Under all, yet not abated—
Thou above—Thy power ordaining—
Thou beneath—Thy strength sustaining—
Thou without—the whole embracing—
Thou within—Thy fullness gracing.
Thee within, no power constraineth—

Extra, nunquam dilataris.
Super, nullo sustentaris;
Subter, nullo fatigaris.
Mundum movens, non moveris;
Locum tenens, non teneris;
Tempus mutans, non mutaris;
Vaga firmans, non vagaris.
Vis externa, vel necesse,
Non alternat tuum esse.
Heri nostrum, cras et pridem,
Semper tibi nunc et idem.
Tuum, Deus, hodiernum
Indivisum, sempiternum;
In hoc, totum prævidisti,
Totum simul perfecisti
Ad exemplar summæ mentis,
Formam præstans elementis.

AD FILIUM.

Nate, Patri coæqualis,
Patri consubstantialis,
Patris splendor, et figura,
Factor factus creatura,
Carnem nostram induisti,
Causam nostram suscepisti.
Sempiternus, temporalis;
Moriturus, immortalis;
Verus homo, verus Deus;
Impermixtus Homo-Deus.

Thou without, no freedom gaineth—
Over all, Thee none sustaineth,
Under all, no burden paineth.
  Moving all, no change Thou knowest—
Holding fast, Thou freely goest.
Changing time, Thou art unchanging
Thou the fickle all arranging.
Force and fate whichever showing
Are but footsteps of Thy going,
Past and future to us, ever
Are to Thee but now forever.
Thy to-day, with Thee abiding
Endless is, no change dividing—
Thou, in it, at once foreseeing
All things, by Thee perfect being,
Like the plan Thy mind completed,
When creation first was meted.

TO THE SON.

  Son, the Father's equal ever,
From His substance changing never,
Like in brightness and in feature,
Though creator, still a creature,
Thou our human body worest
Our redemption too Thou borest.
  Endless, still Thy time declaring,
Deathless, though Thy death preparing,
Man, and God, divided never,
Thou Man-God, unmixed forever,

Non conversus hic in carnem,
Nec minutus propter carnem;
Hic assumptus est in Deum,
Nec consumptus propter Deum;
Patri compar deitate,
Minor carnis veritate.
Deus pater tantum Dei,
Virgo mater est, sed Dei.
 In tam nova ligatura
Sic utraque stat natura,
Ut conservet quicquid erat,
Facta quiddam quod non erat.
 Noster iste Mediator,
Iste noster legis dator;
Circumcisus, baptizatus,
Crucifixus, tumulatus,
Obdormivit, et descendit,
Resurrexit, et ascendit;
Sic ad cœlos elevatus,
Judicabit judicatus.

AD SPIRITUM.

 Paracletus, increatus,
Neque factus, neque natus,
Patri consors genitoque,
Sic procedit ab utroque,
Ne sit minor potestate,
Nec discretus qualitate.
Quanti illi, tantus iste;

God is not to flesh converted,
Nor by flesh the God perverted—
God in human form appearing,
Never human weakness fearing—
With the Father equal being
Fleshly weakness disagreeing,
God the God begetting solely,
Virgin both conceiving wholly.
  In this union, thus created,
Both the natures there are mated,
Each its own existence taking,
Both a new existence making.
  He, alone our Interceder,
Our Lawgiver and our Leader,
He the law and Gospel heeded,
To the cross and grave proceeded,
There He slept and there descended,
There He rose and then ascended.
Judged on earth—in heaven He liveth,
And the world its judgment giveth.

TO THE HOLY SPIRIT.

  Comforter, denominated,
Never born and not created,
Both the Son and Father knowing—
Spirit from them both outgoing,
Thus in power their equal being
And in quality agreeing,
Great as they, He still remaineth,

Quales illi, talis iste;
Ex quo illi, ex tunc iste;
Quantum illi, tantum iste.
  Pater alter, sed gignendo;
Natus alter, sed nascendo;
Flamen, ab his procedendo;
Tres sunt unum, subsistendo.
Quisque trium plenus Deus;
Non tres tamen Di, sed Deus:
In hoc Deo, Deo vero,
Tres et unum assevero;
Dans usiæ unitatem,
Et personis trinitatem.
  In personis, nulla prior,
Nulla major, nulla minor;
Unaquæque semper ipsa,
Sic est constans atque fixa,
Ut nec in se varietur,
Nec in ulla transmutetur.

  Hæc est fides orthodoxa,
Non hic error sine noxa,
Sicut dico, sic et credo,
Nec in pravam partem cedo:
Inde venit, bone Deus,
Ne desperem, quamvis reus,
Reus mortis, non despero,
Sed in morte vitam quæro.
Quo te placem, nil prætendo

All their goodness, he retaineth,
With them from the first existing,
All their power in him subsisting.
Father He begetting showeth,
Son, from human birth He groweth,
Spirit, from them both outflowing,
They are one, the Godhead showing.
Each is God, in fullness ever,
All are God and three Gods never.
In this God, true God completing,
Three in one, are ever meeting,
Unity in substance showing,
Trinity in persons knowing.
Of the persons none is greater,
Neither less and neither later,
Each one still itself retaining,
Fixed and constant still remaining,
In itself no variation,
Neither change, nor transmutation.

This is true faith, for our keeping.
Error bringeth sin and weeping—
As I teach it, I believe it,
Nor for other will I leave it.
Trusting Lord thy goodness ever
Though I sin, I hope forever.
Worthy death, but not despairing,
By my death, my life preparing.
When I please thee, nothing showing

Nisi fidem quam ostendo.
Fidem vides,—hanc imploro,
Leva fascem quo laboro;
Per hoc sacrum cataplasma
Convalescat ægrum plasma.
  Extra portam jam delatum,
Jam fœtentem, tumulatum,
Vitta ligat, lapis urget;
Sed si jubes, hic resurget.
Jube! lapis revolvetur,
Jube! vitta dirumpetur;—
Exiturus nescit moras,
Postquam clamas "Exi foras!"
  In hoc salo, mea ratis
Infestatur a piratis:
Hinc assultus, inde fluctus;
Hinc et inde, mors et luctus;
Sed tu, bone nauta, veni;
Preme ventos, mare leni;
Fac abscedant hi piratæ,
Duc ad portum, salva rate.
  Infœcunda mea ficus;
Cujus ramus, ramus siccus,
Incidetur, incendetur,
Si promulgas quod meretur.
Sed hoc anno dimittatur,
Stercoretur, fodiatur;
Quod si necdum respondebit,—
Flens hoc loquor,—tunc ardebit.

But the faith on Thee bestowing.
Hear my prayer, my faith perceiving,
From my burden, me relieving—
Here, my sickness now revealing,
Let Thy med'cine be my healing.
  Now, without the city taken,
Dead, offensive and forsaken,
Grave clothes bind, the stone confineth—
At Thy word the grave resigneth—
Speak! the stone away is rolling—
Speak! the shroud no more controlling—
When "Come forth" Thy summons sayeth,
Then at once the dead obeyeth.
  On this sea of troubles resting
Pirates are my bark infesting—
Strifes, temptations, billows sweeping,
Everywhere are death and weeping,
Come, Good Pilot, calm proclaiming,
Hush the winds, the billows taming,
Drive these pirates to their hiding,
Safe to port my vessel guiding.
  My unfruitful fig tree growing,
Dry and withered branches showing,
Should'st Thou judge, the truth discerning,
Thou would'st give unto the burning—
But another season bless it,
Dig about it, Lord, and dress it,
If it then no fruit returneth,
I will praise Thee while it burneth.

Vetus hostis in me furit,
Aquis mersat, flammis urit;
Inde languens, et afflictus,
Tibi soli sum relictus.
Ut infirmus convalescat,
Ut hic hostis evanescat,
Tu virtutem jejunandi,
Des infirmo, des orandi;
Per hæc duo, Christo teste,
Liberabor ab hac peste.
Ab hac peste solve mentem,
Fac devotum, pœnitentem;
Da timorem, quo projecto,
De salute nil conjecto;
Da fidem, spem, caritatem;
Da discretam pietatem;
Da contemptum terrenorum,
Appetitum supernorum.

Totum, Deus, in te spero,
Deus, ex te totum quæro;—
Tu laus mea, meum bonum;
Mea cuncta tuum donum.
Tu solamen in labore;
Medicamen in languore;
Tu in luctu mea lyra,
Tu lenimen es in ira;
Tu in arcto liberator;
Tu in lapsu relevator:

Me the Evil one possessing,
Flames and floods by turns oppressing,
Feeble, sick and helpless lying,
To thy grace, my soul is flying.
That my weakness all may vanish,
Thou the evil spirit banish.
Teach me Lord, my weakness staying,
Grace of fasting and of praying,
This alone, the Savior telleth,
Such a demon e'er expelleth.
Thou my sickened sense restoring—
Faith and penitence imploring—
Give me fear which, once ejected,
Leaves salvation all perfected.
Faith and hope and love conferring,
Give me piety, unerring,
Earthly joys forever spurning,
Heavenward still my footsteps turning.

God, in Thee, all things desiring,
From Thee, every thing requiring—
Thou my praise, my good abiding,
All I have, Thy gift providing—
In fatigue, Thy solace feeling,
In my sickness, Thou my healing,
Thou, my harp, my grief assuaging,
Thou who soothest all my raging,
Thou who freest my enthralling,
Thou who raisest me when falling,

Motum præstas in provectu;
Spem conservas in defectu;
Si quis lædit, tu rependis;
Si minatur tu defendis;
Quod est anceps, tu dissolvis;
Quod tegendum, tu involvis.
Tu intrare me non sinas
Infernales officinas,
Ubi mæror, ubi metus;
Ubi fœtor, ubi fletus;
Ubi probra deteguntur,
Ubi rei confunduntur,
Ubi tortor semper cædens,
Ubi vermis semper edens;—
Ubi totum hoc perenne,
Quia perpes mors gehennæ.

Me receptet Sion illa,
Sion, David urbs tranquilla,
Cujus faber, auctor lucis;
Cujus portæ, lignum crucis;
Cujus claves, lingua Petri;
Cujus cives, semper læti;
Cujus muri, lapis vivus;
Cujus custos, Rex festivus.
In hac urbe, lux solemnis;
Ver æternum, pax perennis;
In hac, odor implens cœlos,
In hac, semper festum melos.

'Tis Thy grace my footsteps guideth
Strengthening hope, when it subsideth.
None would hurt, but Thou forefendest,
Who may threaten, Thou defendest,
What is doubtful, Thou revealest,
What is myst'ry, Thou concealest.
Never, Lord, with Thy permission,
Let me enter in perdition,
Where is fear and where is wailing,
Shame and weeping unavailing,
Every loathsome thing displaying,
In confusion, disarraying,
Where the fierce tormentor lieth,
And the worm that never dieth,
Where this endless woe, infernal,
Maketh death and hell eternal.

Let me be in Sion savéd,
Sion, peaceful home of David,
Built by Him, the light who maketh,
And the cross for portals taketh—
And for keys the welcome given
By the joyful saints in Heaven—
Walls of living stone erected,
By the Prince of joy protected—
Where the light, that God is sending,
Endless spring and peace are blending.
Perfume, every breeze is bearing,
Festive strains the joy declaring.

Non est ibi corruptela,
Non defectus, non querela,
Non minuti, non deformes,—
Omnes Christo sunt conformes.
  Urbs cœlestis! urbs beata!
Super petram collocata;—
Urbs in portu satis tuto,
De longinquo, te saluto;—
Te saluto, te suspiro,
Te affecto, te requiro.
  Quantum tui gratulantur,
Quam festive convivantur;
Quis affectus eos stringat,
Aut quæ gemma muros pingat,
Quis chalcedon, quis jacynthus,—
Norunt illi qui sunt intus.
  In plateis hujus urbis,
Sociatus piis turbis,
Cum Moyse et Elija
Pium cantem Halleluia!

No corruption there appeareth,
None defect, or sorrow feareth,
None deformed or dwarfed remaining,
All the form of Christ retaining.
  Heavenly City! happy dwelling!
Built upon that stone excelling.
City safe in heavenly keeping
Hail! in distant glory sleeping!
Thee I hail, for thee am sighing—
Thee I love, for thee am dying.
  How thy heavenly hosts are singing—
And their festive voices ringing—
What the love their souls conforming—
What the gems the walls adorning—
Chalcedon and jacinth shining
Know they all, those walls confining.
  In that City's glorious meeting,
Moses and Elias greeting—
Holy prophets gone before us—
Let me sing the heavenly chorus.

JACOBUS DE BENEDICTIS.

Jacobus de Benedictis, sometimes called Giacomo da Todi, sometimes Giacomo de Benedetti, but more frequently Giacopone, or Jacopone, was an Italian lawyer, of the noble family of the Benedetti, at Todi. The sudden death of his wife at the Theatre, impressed him so powerfully, that he abandoned his successful practice of the law, sold what he had and gave it to the poor, and joined the then young and popular order of the Franciscans and devoted himself to a life of religious austerity. He was extravagant and, if not insane, was sometimes ridiculous in his conduct—in the language of his epitaph "Stultus propter Christum." He attacked with great severity the priestly abuses of his time, for which he suffered a living martyrdom, in the prisons of a bad pope, from which he was finally released. The date of his birth is unknown. He died on Christmas day, 1306, at a great age.

The three poems which I have embraced in this volume, as his, the *Mater Speciosa*, the *Mater Dolorosa* and the *Cur Mundus*, if correctly attributed to him, fully establish his rank as a poet of the greatest merit—and one of them, the *Stabat Mater Dolorosa*, has been admired beyond any other Latin Hymn, except the unapproachable *Dies Iræ*. The Mater Speciosa, is here placed before the Mater Dolorosa, not because I suppose with Dr. Neale that it was the first written, as I do not, but because, in the arrangement which I have adopted, a Hymn of the Nativity should precede one of the Passion. If it had stood alone, or even had it been the first written, it would not have been left to our day to announce its beauties. It seems to me to bear to the Mater Dolorosa, something like the relation of a copy to an original, and thus the excellence and freshness of the original may have kept out of sight the copy, with all its merit, until recent discovery has placed it by the side of its more distinguished sister—if indeed they be by the same author. It is not impossible that the original of the two may have been written by one of the eminent men, earlier than Jacopone, to whom it has been attributed and that the other was but a later imitation.

Those early monks and priests who were really devoted to religion for its own sake and who lived ages before the art of printing, had but few books and of those the Bible was the chief, and their study of it gave them the familiarity with its sacred words, which is so conspicuous in their writings. In this poem, Jacopone while he fully perceives and presents the poetical character of the scene, weaves into his verse, even more than in the Mater Dolorosa, all the striking incidents which the Sacred Record details as part of the wonderful story, and all are enlivened by touches of nature which are as charming as they are truthful.

I am indebted to an interesting article, by Dr. Schaff, under the title "A New Stabat Mater" in the "Hours at Home" for May 1867, for my first sight of this poem. It contains a translation by Neale.

STABAT MATER SPECIOSA.

Stabat Mater speciosa
Juxta fœnum gaudiosa,
  Dum jacebat parvulus—
Cujus animam gaudentem,
Laetabundam ac ferventem,
  Pertransivit jubilus.
O quam læta et beata
Fuit haec immaculata,
  Mater Unigeniti!
Quæ gaudebat et ridebat,
Exultabat, cum videbat
  Nati partum inclyti.
Quis jam est, qui non gauderet
Christi matrem si videret
  In tanto solatio?
Quis non posset collætari,
Christi matrem contemplari,
  Ludentem cum filio?
Pro peccatis suæ gentis,
Christum vidit cum jumentis
  Et algori subditum—

BEAUTIFUL MOTHER BY THE MANGER.

Beautiful, his mother, standing
Near the stall—her soul expanding—
  Saw her new-born lying there—
In her soul, new joy created,
And with holy love elated,
  Rapture glorifying her.
She, her God-begotten greeting,
Felt her spotless bosom beating,
  With a new festivity—
Holy joy, her bosom warming—
Radiant smiles her face conforming—
  At her Son's nativity.
Who could fail to see with pleasure,
Christ's dear mother, without measure
  Such a joy expressing there—
Thus a mother's care beguiling,
Thus beside the manger smiling,
  Her dear Son caressing there?
For the trespass of his nation,
Suffering now humiliation,
  Chilling with the cattle there—

Vidit suum dulcem natum,
Vagientem, adoratum,
  Vili diversorio.
Nato Christo in præsepe,
Cœli cives canunt læte
  Cum immenso gaudio—
Stabat senex cum puella,
Non cum verbo nec loquela,
  Stupescentes cordibus.
Eja mater, fons amoris,
Me sentire vim ardoris,
  Fac ut tecum sentiam!
Fac ut ardeat cor meum
In amatum Christum Deum.
  Ut sibi complaceam.
Sancta mater, istud agas,
Prone introducas plagas
  Cordi fixas valide.
Tui nati cœlo lapsi,
Jam dignati fœno nasci,
  Pœnas mecum divide.
Fac me vere congaudere,
Jesulino cohærere
  Donec ego vixero.
In me sistat ardor tui—
Puerino fac me frui
  Dum sum in exilio.
Hunc ardorem fac communem,
Ne me facias immunem
  Ab hoc desiderio.

Wise men knelt where he was lying,
Still she saw her dear one crying,
  In a cheerless tavern there.
Saviour, cradled in a manger!
Angels hail the heavenly stranger,
  In their great felicity—
Virgin and her husband gazing,
Speechless, saw the sight, amazing,
  Of so great a mystery.
Fount of love, beyond concealing!
May the love which thou art feeling,
  Fill my heart, unceasingly—
Let my heart like thine be glowing—
Holy love of Jesus knowing,
  And, with thee, in sympathy.
Holy mother, for him caring,
Let the ills thy Son is bearing,
  Touch my heart, indelibly—
Of thy Son, from Heaven descended,
In a stable, born and tended,
  Share with me the penalty.
With thee, all thy love dividing,
Be my soul in Christ abiding,
  While this life enchaineth me.
May thy love, my bosom warming,
Make my soul to his conforming,
  While exile detaineth me.
Let my love with thine still blending,
Be for Jesus never ending,
  Nothing e'er restraining me.

Virgo virginum præclara,
Mihi jam non sis amara,
  Fac me parvum rapere,
Fac ut pulchrum fantem portem,
Qui nascendo vicit mortem
  Volens vitam tradere.
Fac me tecum satiari,
Nato me inebriari,
  Stantem in tripudio.
Inflammatus et accensus,
Obstupescit omnis sensus
  Tali de commercio.
Omnes stabulum amantes,
Et pastores vigilantes
  Pernoctantes sociant.
Per virtutem nati tui
Ora ut electi sui
  Ad patriam veniant.
Fac me nato custodiri,
Verbo Dei præmuniri,
  Conservari gratia—
Quando corpus morietur,
Fac ut animæ donetur
  Tui nati visio.

Virgin, first in virgin beauty!
Let me share thy love and duty—
  Clasping, with fidelity,
That dear child, who for us liveth,
By his birth, for death, who giveth
  Life and immortality.
With thee, let me, thrilled with pleasure,
Feel his love, beyond all measure,
  In a sacred dance with thee—
With a holy zeal excited,
Every ravished sense delighted
  In a holy trance with thee.
All who love this sacred manger,
Every watching shepherd stranger,
  All, at night, who come with him—
By thy Son's dear intercession,
May his chosen take possession
  Of his heavenly home with him.
By thy holy Son attended—
By the word of God defended—
  By his grace forgiving me—
When my mortal frame is perished,
May my soul, above be cherished—
  Thy dear Son receiving me.

DE CONTEMPTU MUNDI.

CUR MUNDUS MILITAT.

This poem is but an expansion of this gospel truth, "All flesh is as grass and all the glory of man as the flower "of grass. The grass withereth and the flower thereof "fadeth away, but the Word of the Lord endureth for-"ever." It is now generally attributed to Jacopone (*ante*, p. 18). Up to a few years since it was as generally attributed to St. Bernard. Tusser translated it three hundred years ago, calling it "St. Barnard's Verses." He however gives but eight stanzas, omitting the fourth and the tenth, and they are not arranged as they are in the copy given by Trench. Daniel arranges the stanzas in still another manner and omits the third. I have copied from Trench, but have adopted still another arrangement, as better exhibiting the spirit of the poem. I have also ventured to transpose two words for the sake of the rhythm, reading *Magis credendum est*, instead of *Credendum magis est.* Omissions, errors in arrangement, and false notions of authorship, could not fail to be common, before the art of printing, especially in small poems, which passed from one to another by oral repetition and by manuscript copies, made often by persons who had neither skill nor care in copying.

The following is Tusser's translation:

"Why so triumphs the World, in pomp and glory vain,
Whose state so happy thought, so fickle doth remain?
Whose bravery so slippery stands, and doth so soon
decay,
As doth the potter's pan, compact of brittle clay.
More credit see thou give, to letters wrote in ice,
Than unto vain deceits, of brittle world's device,
In gifts to virtue due, beguiling many one,
Yet those same never have, long time to hope upon.
To false dissembling men, more trust is to be had,
Than to the prosperous state of wretched world so bad.
What with voluptuousness, and other maddish toys,
False studies won with pain, false vanities and joys.
Tell where is Salomon, that once so noble was?
Or where now Samson is, in strength whom none
could pass?
Or worthy Jonathas, that prince so lovely bold?
Or fair Absalom, so goodly to behold?
Shew whither is Cæsar gone, that conquered far and
near?
Or that rich famous carl, so given to belly cheer?
Shew where is Tully now, for eloquence so fit?
Or Aristoteles, of such a pregnant wit?
O thou fit bait for worms! O thou great heap of dust!
O dew! O vanity! why so extoll'st thy lust?
Thou therefore ignorant, what time thou hast to live,
Do good to every man, while here thou hast to give.
How short a feast (to count) is this same world's re-
nown?
Such as men's shadows be, such joy it brings to town,
Which always plucketh us from God's eternal bliss,
And leadeth man to hell, a just reward of his.
The bravery of this world, esteemed here so much,
In Scripture likened is to flowers of grass and such,
Like as the leaf so light, which wind abroad doth
blow,
So doth this worldly life, the life of man bestow."

DE CONTEMPTU MUNDI.

Cur mundus militat sub vana gloria,
Cujus prosperitas est transitoria?
Jam cito labitur ejus potentia,
Quam vasa figuli, quæ sunt fragilia.

Plus fide literis scriptis in glacie,
Quam mundi fragilis vanæ fallaciæ,
Fallax in præmiis, virtutis specie,
Qui nunquam habuit tempus fiduciæ.

Magis credendum est viris fallacibus,
Quam mundi miseris prosperitatibus,
Falsis insaniis et vanitatibus,
Falsisque studiis et voluptatibus.

Tot clari proceres, tot rerum spatia,
Tot ora praesulum, tot regna fortia,
Tot mundi principes, tanta potentia,
In ictu oculi, clauduntur omnia.

Dic, ubi Salomon, olim tam nobilis,
Vel ubi Samson est, dux invincibilis,
Vel pulcher Absalom, vultu mirabilis,
Vel dulcis Jonathas, multum amabilis?

CONTEMPT OF THE WORLD.

Why does the world serve the glory it cherisheth,
Since its prosperity all surely perisheth,
Passing away with its strength and ability,
Quickly as pottery, with its fragility?

Think that a record on ice may be permanent,
More than the fallacies under the firmament,
False in rewards, without virtue or verity,
Never the world hath a time for sincerity.

Far better trust men of falsehood, deceiving thee,
Than the vain world that forever is giving thee
Pleasures that vanish and foolish insanities,
Studies delusive and perishing vanities.

Nobles and prelates, in all ages flourishing—
Pride and dominion and vainglory nourishing—
Kings of the earth, with their power and stability—
All, at a glance, show the end of nobility.

Where now is Solomon, learnéd and glorious?
Where now is Samson, so strong and victorious?
Where, too, is Absalom, princely and beautiful?
Jonathan, loving and lovely and dutiful?

Quo Cæsar abiit, celsus imperio,
Vel Dives splendidus, totus in prandio?
Dic, ubi Tullius, clarus eloquio,
Vel Aristoteles, summus ingenio?

Quam breve festum est hæc mundi gloria!
Ut umbra hominis, sic ejus gaudia,
Quæ semper subtrahunt æterna præmia,
Et ducunt hominem ad dura devia.

O esca vermium! O massa pulveris!
O ros, O vanitas, cur sic extolleris?
Ignorans penitus, utrum cras vixeris,
Fac bonum omnibus, quamdiu poteris.

Hæc carnis gloria, quæ tanti penditur,
Sacris in literis, flos fœni dicitur—
Ut leve folium, quod vento rapitur,
Sic vita hominis luci subtrahitur.

Nil tuum dixeris quod potes perdere,
Quod mundus tribuit, intendit rapere—
Superna cogita, cor sit in æthere,
Felix, qui potuit mundum contemnere!

Where now is Cæsar, so proud and imperious?
Dives the sumptuous, rich and luxurious?
Say, where is Cicero, famous and eloquent?
Where Aristotle, in genius preëminent?

World of vainglory, a vanishing festival!
How like the shadows pass pleasures terrestrial!
Robbing the soul of its hopes and its purity—
Leading man on to a woeful futurity.

Food of the worm! Here thy dust is the most of thee!
Vanishing dew-drop! O why do they boast of thee!
Ignorant soul! thy to-morrow may perish thee,
Then, while thou canst, do the good that may cherish thee.

Pride of the flesh, which thou thinkest so dearly of!
Flower of the grass, which the Word speaketh clearly of!
Like the dead leaf, which the autumn wind scattereth,
So passeth life, with the vain hope that flattereth.

Call nothing thine, which so quickly may break away;
What the world giveth, it meaneth to take away;
Think on the skies, set thy heart on eternity—
Happy, despising this world of infirmity!

THE DAY OF JUDGMENT.

THIS old alphabetic poem is of a very early period, at least as early as the seventh century, being referred to by Bede, who died early in the eighth century. The author's name has been lost in the ages.

It is more properly narrative than lyrical, and lacks polish and grace; but this is more than made up by its simplicity and solemnity. Having been written before the *Dies Iræ*, it has been supposed to have suggested that majestic and solitary hymn, but with slight reason. The topic and the scene are different, as well as the instruction and the spirit of the whole piece. That is but the natural and agonizing expression of penitence and prayer by an individual sinner, in view of the awful solemnities of the final day of wrath. This is a noble, simple and trusting paraphrase of the 29th and 30th verses of the 24th chapter of Matthew and of the 31st to the 45th verses of the 25th chapter, which contain a striking account of a trial at the Judgment—the organization of the court, the summons, the complaint, the trial, the judgment, the execution, so circumstantially and solemnly reported by the Judge Himself, that it is impossible to doubt that it was intended to convey to us a lively and instructive representation of the circumstances and manner of the final Judgment, and, in the most forcible manner, to teach us, as His life had done, that when He shall come to judge every man according to his works, it will be a life of goodness and love of Christ, which will be the test of pure religion and undefiled before God and the Father.

DE DIE JUDICII.

Apparebit repentina dies magna Domini,
Fur obscura velut nocte improvisos occupans.
Brevis totus tunc parebit prisci luxus sæculi,
Totum simul cum clarebit præterisse sæculum.
Clangor tubæ per quaternas terræ plagas concinens,
Vivos una mortuosque Christo ciet obviam.
De celesti Judex arce, majestate fulgidus,
Claris angelorum choris comitatus aderit.
Erubescet orbis lunæ, sol vel obscurabitur,
Stellæ cadent pallescentes, mundi tremet ambitus—
Flamma ignis anteibit justi vultum Judicis,
Cœlum, terras, et profundi fluctus ponti devorans.
Gloriosus in sublimi Rex sedebit solio,

THE DAY OF JUDGMENT.

At the last, the great day of the Lord shall arise,
As a thief in the night, to dismay and surprise.
Then how transient will seem all the pleasures of earth,
When the end of all time shall be past, like its birth—
When the trumpet shall call from all quarters below,
Both the quick and the dead to the judgment to go.
From his heavenly palace, majestic and bright,
Shall the Judge, with His angels, come glorious in light,
While the sun shall be dark and the moon be like blood,
And the stars fade and fall, and earth shake like a flood.
From the face of the Judge shall the flame of his ire,
All the air and the earth and the sea, burn with fire.
And the King shall then sit on his throne in the sky,

Angelorum tremebunda circumstabunt agmina.
Hujus omnes ad electi collegentur dexteram,
Pravi pavent a sinistris, hædi velut fœtidi—
Ita dicet Rex ad dextros, regnum cœli sumite,
Pater orbis quod paravit ante omne sæculum.
Karitate qui fraterna me juvistis pauperem.
Caritatis nunc mercedem reportate divites.
Laeti dicent Quando, Christe, pauperem te vidimus,
Te, Rex magne, vel egentem miserati juvimus,
Magnus illis dicet Judex—Cum juvistis pauperem,
Panem, domum, vestem dantes, me juvistis humiles.
Nec tardabit et sinistris loqui justus Arbiter—
In gehennæ, maledicti, flammas hinc discedite,
Obsecrantem me audire despexistis mendicum,
Nudo vestem non dedistis, neglexistis languidum.

And all of His angels stand worshipping by.
To His right His elect He shall call by His grace,
While the wicked, like goats, on the left He shall place.
Then to those on His right hand the King shall declare,
"Take the kingdom my Father for you did prepare—
For 'twas when I was poor that your love gave me aid—
From the riches of love your reward now is made."
Then the righteous shall ask, "When, oh Lord, did we bless
Thee, our heavenly King, or relieve Thy distress?"
And the Judge shall reply, "When the poor ye did heed,
Giving shelter and clothing and bread for their need."
And to those on His left shall the Just Judge proclaim,
"Ye accursèd, depart to unquenchable flame;
Ye despised me when I for your alms did implore,
Being sick and forsaken and naked and sore."

Peccatores dicent—Christe, quando te vel pauperem,
Te Rex magne vel infirmum contemplantes sprevimus?
Quibus contra Judex altus—Mendicanti quamdiu
Opem ferre despexistis, me sprevistis improbi.
Retro ruent tum injusti ignes in perpetuos,
Vermis quorum non morietur, flamma nec restinguitur,
Satan atro cum ministris quo tenetur carcere,
Fletus ubi mugitusque strident omnes dentibus.
Tunc fideles ad cœlestem sustollentur patriam,
Choros inter angelorum regni petent gaudia,
Urbis summae Hierusalem introibunt gloriam,
Vera lucis atque pacis in qua fulget visio.
Xristum Regem, jam paterna claritate splendidum,
Ubi celsa beatorum contemplantur agmina.
Ydri fraudes ergo cave, infirmantes subleva,

And the wicked shall say, "Lord, oh when did we
 spurn
Thee, O King, and away from thy poverty
 turn?"
"This to me ye have done," then the great Judge
 shall say,
"When the poor ye despised and from him turned
 away."
And then back shall they rush to the flames that
 arise,
Where the fire is not quenched and their worm
 never dies—
Where the devil is bound in his prison be-
 neath—
Where are weeping and groaning and gnashing of
 teeth.
Then the faithful shall rise to their heavenly
 home,
In the joys of the kingdom with angels to
 roam,
They shall enter the bliss of the city of God—
Where the visions of peace and of light shine
 abroad—
Where the throngs of the blessèd Christ Jesus
 adore,
As He shineth in glory His Father before.
Shun the wiles of the serpent, give aid to the
 weak,

Aurum temne, fuge luxus, si vis astra
petere—
Zona clara castitatis lumbos nunc ac-
cingere,
In occursum magni Regis fer ardantes
lampades.

Flee thy worldly desires, if the skies thou wouldst seek.
And begird up thy loins, with a zone pure and white;
Be prepared for the King, with thy lamps burning bright.

VENI, CREATOR SPIRITUS.

THIS HYMN has always been held in the highest estimation as an invocation of that Creative Spirit which gives the birth of a new spiritual life. "That which is born of the spirit is spirit." From its use as a prayer for the regeneration of the new birth it passed easily into use, in the Roman Catholic Church, as an appointed song for those sacred and solemn occasions where the blessing of the Spirit is invoked upon one about to enter upon a new life, in which the divine aid is especially necessary, as in the ordering of priests, the consecration of bishops and archbishops, and the coronation of kings and popes. It is also used as a Pentecostal hymn. There is a translation of it in the Book of Common Prayer of the Episcopal Church, in the Form for ordering priests. It is, however, more properly a paraphrase than a translation—the seven stanzas of the original being expanded into sixteen.

Its authorship is commonly attributed to Charlemagne, who died in the year 814. I adopt, however, the opinion of Trench, that it is certainly older than the time of that great monarch. Judging from internal evidence alone, I should not hesitate to ascribe it to St. Ambrose, who died in 397. I give but little importance to the ascription of it to Charlemagne. It may very well be but one of the many examples of the facility with which opinions on such matters, once expressed, even without evidence, are repeated until they are generally believed, no one taking the trouble to inquire into their foundation. The high character and various talents of St. Ambrose—"*Doctor Mellifluus et Mellitissimus,*" as he was called—caused to be attributed to him many hymns of great antiquity, of which he was finally believed not to be the author, the effect of which was to make many believe that there are no hymns which can with certainty be said to be his, and I know of no authority for saying that this is his. Except as a matter of literary history, it is of little importance who was the author. The merit of the hymn is in itself alone. Its comprehensiveness and brevity, its simplicity and beauty, its gentle spirit of trust and devotion, and its earnest directness of expression, mark it as the production of a great and practised writer and a devout Christian, studiously familiar with the Scriptures and with theological truth, rather than of a proud monarch and a great soldier.

VENI, CREATOR SPIRITUS.

Veni, creator Spiritus,
Mentes tuorum visita,
Imple superna gratia
Quæ tu creasti pectora.
Qui diceris paracletus,
Altissimi donum Dei,
Fons vivus, ignis, caritas,
Et spiritalis unctio.
Tu septiformis munere,
Digitus paternæ dextræ,
Tu rite promissum Patris,
Sermone ditans guttura.
Accende lumen sensibus,
Infunde amorem cordibus,
Infirma nostri corporis
Virtute firmans perpeti.
Hostem repellas longius,
Pacemque dones protinus;
Ductore sic te prævio,
Vitemus omne noxium.
Per te sciamus da Patrem,
Noscamus atque Filium;

COME, CREATIVE SPIRIT.

SPIRIT, heavenly life bestowing,
Spirit, all Thy new-born knowing,
Fill with gracious inspiration
Every soul of Thy creation.
Comforter from God descending,
Life and unction ever blending—
Fount of living waters flowing,
Flame of love for ever glowing.
Sevenfold, precious gifts conferring,
Finger of the Lord, unerring—
Promise, by the Father given,
Teacher of the speech of heaven—
For our senses light securing,
Fill our hearts with love enduring;
In our bodies strength implanting,
Faith and firmness ever granting.
Far the foe to grace repelling,
Give us endless peace indwelling;
Thou, as leader, deign to guide us,
That no evil may betide us.
By Thy grace the Father learning,
And the blessed Son discerning;

Te utriusque Spiritum
Credamus omni tempore.
  Gloria Patri Domino,
Natoque qui a mortuis
Surrexit, ac Paraclito,
In sæculorum sæcula.

Thee, of both the spirit blending,
Let us trust through life unending.
To the God who being gave us,
To the Son who rose to save us,
To the Spirit sanctifying,
Glory be through life undying!

COME, CREATIVE SPIRIT.

ANOTHER VERSION.

SPIRIT creative, power divine!
Visit every soul of Thine,
Give the hearts that Thou hast made,
Thy celestial grace and aid.
Fount where living waters flow,
Flame of heavenly love below,
Holy Ghost, by God conferred,
Unction of the living Word,
Sending seven-fold gifts abroad,
Finger of the hand of God,
Promise of the Father's grace,
Gift of speech in every place,
Let our senses feel Thy flame,
Strengthen Thou our mortal frame.
In our hearts Thy love bestow,
Faith and firmness let us know.
Far the foe to grace repel,
Let Thy peace within us dwell,
Guide our feet Thy race to run,
Teach us every ill to shun.
Make us all the Father know,
And the blessed Son below,

Give us endless faith in Thee,
Spirit of the sacred Three!
Glory to the Father be,
Glory to the risen Son,
Glory, Holy Ghost, to Thee,
While eternal ages run.

COME, CREATIVE SPIRIT.

ANOTHER VERSION.

Come Thou Spirit, life bestowing,
Inwardly Thy new-born knowing—
Fount of living waters flowing—
Flame of love, forever glowing—
Comforter from God descending,
Life and unction ever blending,
Fill with grace of Thine own sending,
Every heart on Thee depending.
Thou Thy seven-fold gifts providing,
Thou God's hand our footsteps guiding,
Thou His promise still abiding,
To our lips His word confiding,
For our senses light securing,
Fill our hearts with love enduring,
All the body's weakness curing,
Faith and strength in us maturing.
Far the foe to grace repelling,
Give us endless peace indwelling,
Leader Thou, our pathway telling,
Every evil thing dispelling.
Us unto the Father leading
And the Saviour interceding,

In Thyself, from both proceeding,
Give the faith that we are needing.
To the Father, life supplying,
To the Son, for sinners dying,
To the Spirit sanctifying,
Glory be through life undying!

THE LAST SUPPER—ST. THOMAS AQUINAS.

St. Thomas Aquinas, born in 1224, of a noble family, was one of the most illustrious saints of the Roman Catholic Church. He was remarkable for his learning, his eloquence, and his ability as an instructor in letters and religion, and his eminent piety—excelling all his contemporaries. His friendship was sought by the most distinguished men of his time, and he was offered the dignities of the church; but these he steadily refused to accept. He could not, however, prevent them from calling him the *Doctor Angelicus.* When Pope Urban IV. determined to establish the festival of the Holy Sacrament, he directed this learned and pious divine to prepare the "office" for that day. He composed the celebrated lyrics, *Pange, Lingua, Gloriosi* and *Lauda, Sion, Salvatorem,* as the hymn and the prose for that solemn service. Both of them stand in the second rank among the hymns of the mediæval period, the *Dies Iræ* alone holding the first.

They are excluded from the collection of Trench because of their seeming to teach the Roman Catholic doctrine of transubstantiation. The language of this hymn, of the Last Supper, is not, however, subject to any objection on this ground, which would not apply to that of the Saviour in the institution of the Supper, and to his instructions in the sixth chapter of John, which are not only consistent with our faith, but are, indeed, the foundation of it. The Protestant faith on this subject is well expressed and proved by Lady Jane Grey, in her interview with Dr. Feckenham, who had been sent by Queen Mary to convert her to the Catholic religion.

"*Feckenham.* Do you not receive the very body and blood of Christ?

Lady Jane. No, surely, I do not so believe. I think that, at the Supper, I neither receive flesh nor blood, but bread and wine, which bread, when it is broken, and which wine, when it is drunken, putteth me in remembrance how that, for my sins, the body of Christ was broken and his blood shed on the cross; and with that bread and wine I receive the benefits that came by the breaking of his body and shedding his blood for our sins on the cross.

" *Feckenham.* Why, doth not Christ speak these words, 'Take, eat, this is my body?' Doth he not say it is his body?

"*Lady Jane.* I grant he saith so, and so he saith I am the vine, I am the door; but he is never more the door or the vine. I pray you to answer me to this one question. Where was Christ when he said, 'Take, eat, this is my body?' Was he not at the table when he said so? He was at that time alive, and suffered not till the next day. What took he but bread? What brake he but bread? Look, what he took he brake; and look, what he brake he gave; and look, what he gave they did eat. And yet all this time he himself was alive and at supper, before his disciples."

PANGE, LINGUA, GLORIOSI.

Pange, lingua, gloriosi
Corporis mysterium,
Sanguinisque pretiosi,
Quem in mundi pretium,
Fructus ventris generosi,
Rex effudit gentium.
Nobis datus, nobis natus
Ex intacta Virgine,
Et in mundo conversatus,
Sparso verbi semine,
Sui moras incolatus
Miro clausit ordine.
In supremæ nocte cœnæ,
Recumbens cum fratribus,
Observata lege plene
Cibis in legalibus,
Cibum turbæ duodenæ
Se dat suis manibus.
Verbum caro, panem verum
Verbo carnem efficit:
Fitque sanguis Christi merum;
Et si sensus deficit,

SING, MY TONGUE.

Sing, my tongue, the theme undying,
  Mystery which His Body knoweth;
Precious blood of crucifying,
  Which the world's Redeemer showeth;
Fruit of heavenly sanctifying,
  Whence the world's redemption floweth.
From the Blessed Virgin going,
  He with men on earth resided;
Sacred seed for ever sowing,
  He the fruit to us confided;
Till His end, His triumph showing,
  He His wondrous sojourn guided.
In the night of His last meeting,
  With His brethren there united,
All the Paschal forms completing,
  By the ancient law indited,
Him He offered for their eating,
  And His dying love recited.
Word made flesh, among us dwelling,
  With true bread and wine regaleth;
By His word the mystery telling—
  And if sense imperfect faileth—

Ad firmandum cor sincerum
Sola fides sufficit.
  Tantum ergo Sacramentum
Veneremur cernui;
Et antiquum documentum
Novo cedat ritui,
Præstet fides supplementum
Sensuum defectui.
  Genitori, genitoque
Laus et jubilatio,
Salus, honor, virtus quoque
Sit et benedictio:
Procedenti ab utroque
Compar sit laudatio.

From the true heart, doubt dispelling,
  Still the trust of faith prevaileth.
Such a sacrament provided,
  Bowed and humble let us take it;
Rites to ancient times confided,
  Yield to what the new rites make it;
Be not by the sense misguided,
  But in humble faith partake it.
Father, God of our salvation!
  Son, for sinners interceding!
Holy Ghost, our renovation,
  Spirit, from them both proceeding!
To the Three be jubilation,
  Honor, praise, and joy exceeding!

DE PASSIONE DOMINI.

Ecquis binas columbinas
Alas dabit animæ?
Ut in almam crucis palmam
Evolet citissime,
In qua Jesus totus laesus,
Orbis desiderium,
Et immensus est suspensus,
Factus improperium!
Oh cor, scande—Jesu, pande
Caritatis viscera,
Et profunde me reconde
Intra sacra vulnera—
In superna me caverna
Colloca maceriæ—
Hic viventi, quiescenti
Finis est miseriæ!
O mi Deus, amor meus!
Tune pro me pateris?
Pro indigno, crucis ligno,
Jesu mi, suffigeris?
Pro latrone, Jesu bone,
Tu in crucem tolleris?

59

THE PASSION OF THE LORD.

Oh! had it the wings of a dove,
  Quick my soul would to Calvary fly,
And light on the cross of His love,
  Where they've nailed the Redeemer to die:
Where Jesus, the hope of the earth,
  By their cruelty, bleeding and torn,
And crowned as a sport for their mirth,
  All their scoffs and derision has borne.
Oh! rise then, my heart, and away;
  Where Thy yearning, dear Jesus, abounds,
There now in Thy love let me stay,
  Let me hide in the depth of Thy wounds.
On high, in the home of the blest,
  In the cleft of the Rock give me peace,
Where dwelling, my spirit may rest,
  And my trouble and misery cease.
Oh! tell me, my Love and my God,
  If indeed Thou art suff'ring for me?
For me hast to Calvary trod,
  And dost hang on the merciless tree?
With thieves, Lord of goodness and grace,
  Have Thine enemies crucified Thee?

Pro peccatis meis gratis,
Vita mea, moreris?
Non sum tanti, Jesu quanti
Amor tuus æstimat—
Heu! cur ego vitam dego
Si cor te non redamat?
Benedictus sit invictus
Amor vincens omnia,
Amor fortis, tela mortis
Reputans ut somnia.
Iste fecit et refecit
Amor, Jesu, perditum.
O insignis, Amor, ignis
Cor accende frigidum!
O fac vere cor ardere
Fac me te diligere—
Da conjungi, da defungi
Tecum, Jesu, vivere!

My sins dost Thou bear in my place?
  And, my Life, art Thou dying for me?
O Jesus! unworthy am I—
  Undeserving the love Thou hast shown.
Ah! what does this life signify,
  If my heart do not love like Thine own?
The love that o'er all doth prevail,
  Let it blest and unconquered remain,
And death and his darts that assail
  Be but dreams that are transient and vain.
This love that has made us Thine own,
  Blessèd Saviour, the lost doth reclaim;
The warmth of that love make it known,
  Till it kindle my heart with its flame.
My heart, let it burn with Thy love;
  With a holy desire let me sigh,
To join with my Saviour above,
  And to dwell with Thee, Jesus, on high.

STABAT MATER DOLOROSA.

The most striking poetical situation in sacred history is the Mother of Jesus at the Cross. It could not fail to be the subject of a mediæval hymn. The world-renowned *Stabat Mater* is that hymn, which, after being ascribed to many eminent authors, is now commonly attributed to Jacopone (ante, page 18). "The mysterious charm and power of the hymn is due to the subject, and to the intensity of feeling with which the author has seized it. Mary stood there not only as the mother, but as the representative of the whole Christian church, for which the eternal Son of God suffered the most ignominious death on the cross. The author had the rare poetic faculty to bring out, as from immediate vision and heartfelt sympathy, the deep meaning of these scenes, in stanzas of classic beauty and melody that melt the heart and start the tear of penitential grief at the cross of Christ."

"The *Mater Dolorosa* has been regarded by universal consent as the most pathetic and touching of Latin church lyrics, and inferior only to the *Dies Iræ*, which stands alone in its glory and overpowering effect. Daniel calls it the queen of sequences. It breathes the spirit of profound repentance and glowing love, such as can be kindled only by long and intense contemplation of the mystery of the cross—that most amazing and affecting spectacle ever presented to the gaze of heaven and earth. The agony of Mary at the cross, and the sword which then pierced through her soul, according to the prophecy of Simeon, never found more perfect expression. It surpasses in effect the *Mater Dolorosas* of the greatest painters. The key-note of the hymn is contained in the first two lines, and is suggested by the brief but pregnant sentence of St. John, *Stabat juxta crucem mater ejus.* Vulg. It is brought out with overpowering effect in the Hymn, as has been felt even by those who have little religious sympathy with the theme. 'The loveliness of sorrow,' says Tieck, 'in the depth of pain, the smiling in tears, the childlike simplicity which touches on the highest heaven, had to me never before risen so bright in the soul. I had to turn away to hide my tears, especially at the place, '*Vidit suum dulcem natum.*'"

"The *Mater Dolorosa* has furnished the text of some of the noblest musical compositions by Palestrina, Pergolesi, Astorga, Haydn, Bellini, Rossini, Neukomm. That of Palestrina is still annually performed in the Sistine Chapel, during Passion week.

"There are about eighty translations of this hymn in German, and there are several in English; but very few of those in English preserve the original metre."

The foregoing quotations are from the admirable article of Dr. Schaff, in the "Hours at Home," to which I have elsewhere referred.

STABAT MATER DOLOROSA.

Stabat Mater dolorosa
Juxta crucem lacrymosa,
Dum pendebat Filius—
Cujus animam gementem,
Contristantem & dolentem,
Pertransibit gladius.
O quam tristis & afflicta
Fuit illa benedicta,
Mater Unigeniti!
Quæ mœrebat, & dolebat,
Et tremebat cum videbat
Nati pœnas inclyti!
Quis est homo qui non fleret,
Christi Matrem si videret
In tanto supplicio?
Quis posset non contristari
Piam Matrem contemplari,
Dolentem cum Filio?
Pro peccatis suæ gentis,
Vidit Jesum in tormentis,
Et flagellis subditum.
Vidit suum dulcem Natum,
Morientem, desolatum,
Dum emisit spiritum

WEEPING STOOD HIS MOTHER.

Weeping stood His mother, sighing
By the cross where Jesus, dying,
Hung aloft on Calvary;
Through her soul, in sorrow moaning,
Bowed in grief, in spirit groaning,
Pierced the sword in misery.
Filled with grief beyond all others,
Mother—blessed among mothers—
Of the God-begotten one!
How she sorroweth and grieveth,
Trembling as she thus perceiveth
Dying her unspotted one!
Who could there refrain from weeping,
Seeing Christ's dear mother keeping,
In her grief, so bitterly?
Who could fail to share her anguish,
Seeing thus the mother languish,
Lost in woe so utterly?
For the trespass of his nation
She beheld his laceration,
By their scourges suffering.
She beheld her dearest taken,
Crucified, and God-forsaken,
Dying by their torturing.

Eia Mater fons amoris,
Me sentire vim doloris,
Fac ut tecum lugeam.
Fac ut ardeat cor meum
In amando Christum Deum,
Ut sibi complaceam.
Sancta Mater, istud agas,
Crucifixi fige plagas
Cordi meo valide.
Tui Nati vulnerati,
Jam dignati pro me pati,
Pœnas mecum divide.
Fac me vere tecum flere,
Crucifixo condolere,
Donec ego vixero.
Juxta Crucem tecum stare,
Te libenter sociare,
In planctu desidero.
Virgo virginum præclara,
Mihi jam non sis amara,
Fac me tecum plangere.
Fac ut portem Christi mortem,
Passionis ejus sortem
Et plagas recolere.
Fac me plagis vulnerari,
Cruce hac inebriari,
Ob amorem Filii.
Inflammatus & accensus,
Per te, Virgo, sim defensus
In die judicii.

Mother, fountain of affection,
Let me share thy deep dejection,
    Let me share thy tenderness;
Let my heart, thy sorrow feeling,
Love of Christ, the Lord, revealing,
    Be like thine in holiness!
All His stripes, oh! let me feel them,
On my heart for ever seal them,
    Printed there enduringly.
All His woes, beyond comparing,
For my sake in anguish bearing,
    Let me share them willingly.
By thy side let me be weeping,
True condolence with him keeping,
    Weeping all my life with thee;
Near the cross with thee abiding,
Freely all thy woes dividing,
    In thy sorrow joined with thee.
Virgin, of all virgins fairest,
Let me feel the love thou bearest,
    Sharing all thy suffering;
Let me feel the death they gave Him,
Crucified in shame to save them,
    Dying without murmuring.
Let me feel their blows so crushing,
Let me drink the current gushing
    From His wounds when crucified.
By a heavenly zeal excited,
When the judgment fires are lighted.
    Then may I be justified.

Fac me Cruce custodiri,
Morte Christi præmuniri,
Confoveri gratia.
Quando corpus morietur,
Fac ut animæ donetur
Paradisi gloria.

On the Cross of Christ relying,
Through His death redeemed from dying,
By His favor fortified;
When my mortal frame is perished,
Let my spirit then be cherished,
And in heaven be glorified.

DE CORONA SPINEA.

Si vis vere gloriari,
Et a Deo coronari
  Honore et gloria,
Hanc coronam contemplari
Studeas, atque sectari
  Portantis vestigia.
Hanc Cœlorum Rex portavit,
Honoravit et sacravit
  Sacro suo capite—
In hac galea pugnavit,
Cum antiquum hostem stravit,
  Triumphans in stipite.
Haec pugnantis galea,
Triumphantis laurea,
  Tiara pontificis—
Primum fuit spinea,
Postmodum fit aurea
  Tactu sancti verticis.
Spinarum aculeos
Virtus fecit aureos
  Christi passionis.
Quæ peccatis spineos
Mortis æternæ reos,
  Adimplevit bonis.

THE CROWN OF THORNS.

Woulds't thy spirit glory truly—
By the Lord be honored duly,
    With a crown irradiate,
Think upon the crown they gave Him,
Crucified in scorn to save them—
    Strive His life to imitate.
This, the King of Heaven, dying,
Honoring and sanctifying,
    Wore in shame and misery.
In this helmet He contended,
When His strife in triumph ended,
    On the cross of Calvary.
Helmet which the soldier beareth—
Laurel which the victor weareth—
    High priest's mitre, consecrate—
First of thorns His temples tearing,
Then of gold beyond comparing,
    By His touching transmutate.
Thorns He wore amid their scorning,
Change to gold His brows adorning—
    By the death He suffereth.
Which to those by sin perverted—
From eternal death converted—
    Every blessing offereth.

De malis colligitur
Et de spinis plectitur
  Spinea perversis.
Sed in aurum vertitur,
Quando culpa tollitur,
  Eisdem conversis.
Jesu pie, Jesu bone,
Nostro nobis in agone
  Largere victoriam—
Mores nostros sic compone
Ut perpetuæ coronæ
  Mereamur gloriam.

Thorns, by wicked hands collected,
In a plaited crown connected,
    Pierce the wicked bearing it;
When away our sin He taketh,
This a crown of gold He maketh,
    To his children wearing it.
Jesus in Thy goodness aid us—
In the strife that sin has made us,
    Give us, Lord, the victory.
So our daily lives preparing,
That, Thine endless glory sharing,
    We may wear the crown with Thee.

VICTIMÆ PASCHALI LAUDES.

THE FOUR PRINCIPAL PROSES.

This hymn, of which the author is unknown, is said every day of Easter week. It is one of the four principal Proses of the Roman Catholic books of devotion. They were called *Sequences*, from their place in the services of the Roman Catholic Church—they followed the Gradual. They were called *proses*, because they were not verse in the classical sense, but prose; that is to say, they disregarded the quantitative measure of the classical poets, and, in place of it, substituted syllabic measure and accentual rhythm.

"*Prose*, nom qu'on a donné dans les derniers siècles a certaines hymnes composées de vers sans mesure, mais de certain nombre de syllabes avec des rimes qui se chantent après le graduel, d'où on les à aussi appellées sequence—sequentia, c'est à dire qui suit après le graduel."—*Supp. Morer.*

"*Prose* se dit aussi d'une sorte d'ouvrage latin en rimes, ou sans observer la quantité, on observe le nombre des syllabes. On chante à la messe, immediatement avant l'evangile, quelques ouvrages de cette nature dans les solemnités."—*Dict. Acad.*

"*Prosa*, that which is not metre."—*Holyoke Lat. Dict.*

Although at the first the rhyme and the rhythm were

both imperfect, in the course of time the versification and the rhyme were alike regular and harmonious.

"L'usage des proses a commencé au plus tard au neuvième siècle. Notker, moine de S. Gal, qui écrivit vers l'an 880, et qui est regardé comme le premier auteur que l'on connaisse, en fait de proses, dit dans la préface du livre où il en parle qui il en avoit vu dans un antiphonier de l'abbaye de Jumieges, laquelle fut brulée par les Normands en 841. Nous avons quatre *proses* principales, le *Veni, Sancte Spiritus*, pour la Pentecôte, que Durand attribue au Roi Robert, mais qui est plus probablement de *Hermannus Contractus*—c'est la prose *Sancti Spiritus adsit nobis gratia*, qui est du roi Robert, selon quelques anciens, entr' autres Brompton plus ancien que Durand—Le *Lauda Sion salvatorem*, pour la fête du S. Sacrement qui est de S. Thomas d'Aquin—Le *Victimæ paschali laudes* dont on ignore l'auteur—c'est la prose du temps de Pâques—Le *Dies iræ, Dies illa*, que l'on chante aux services des morts. On l'attribue mal àpropos à S. Grégoire, ou à S. Bernard, ou à Humbert, général des dominicains. Cette prose est du Cardinal Frangipani, dit Malabranca, docteur de Paris, de l'ordre des dominicains qui mourut à Perouse en 1294."—*Encyc. et Supp. Morer.*

The *Victimæ paschali laudes* is usually printed in the form of prose, as I give it. I do not doubt, however, that its author considered it a rhymed lyric—poetical in its thought and conception, but really written in prosaic form, and interspersed, at unequal intervals, with rhymes of a very irregular and imperfect character, furnishing an apt illustration of the remarks of Archbishop Trench on the infancy and progress of Latin rhymed accentual versification. He says (I abridge his remarks): 'Rhyme made itself an occasional place even in the later or prosodic poetry of Rome, but no large employment of it dates higher than the eighth or ninth centuries. It displayed itself first in lines which, having a little relaxed the strictness of metrical observance, sought to find a compensation for this in similar closes to the verse, being at this time very far from that elaborate and perfect instrument which it afterwards became. We may trace it, step by step, from its rude, timid, and uncertain beginnings, till, in the later hymnologists of the twelfth and thirteenth centuries, an Aquinas or an Adam of St. Victor, it displayed all its latent capabilities, and attained its final glory and perfection, satiating the ear with a richness of melody scarcely anywhere to be surpassed. At first the rhymes were often merely vowel or assonant ones, the consonants not being required to agree; or the rhyme was adhered to when this was convenient, but disregarded when the needful word was not at hand; or the stress of the rhyme was suffered to fall on an unaccented syllable, thus scarcely striking the ear; or it was limited to the similar termination of a single letter; while sometimes, on the strength of this like ending, as sufficiently sustaining the melody, the whole other construction of the verse and arrangement of the syllables was neglected. It may be that they who first used it, were oftentimes scarcely, or not at all, conscious of what they were doing.'

The following arrangement of the whole original hymn illustrates these remarks:

Victimæ Paschali,
Laudes immolent Christiani,
Agnus redemit oves,
Christus innocens Patri
Reconciliavit peccatores.
Mors et vita, duello,
Conflixere mirando.
Dux vitæ mortuus,
Regnat vivus.
Dic nobis, Maria,
Quid vidisti in via?
Sepulcrum Christi viventis
Et gloriam vidi resurgentis.
Dic nobis, Maria
Quid vidisti in via?
Angelicos testes,
Sudarium et vestes.
Dic nobis, Maria,
Quid vidisti in via.
Surrexit Christus, spes mea.
Præcedet suos in Galilæam.
Credendum est magis soli Mariæ veraci,
Quam Judæorum turbæ fallaci.
Scimus Christum surrexisse à mortuis vere,
Tu nobis victor, Rex miserere.

Thus arranged, at its full length, it gives strong color to the suggestion, which has been made, that, originally, it had a dramatic character, and was sung, responsively, by a choir and by persons representing Mary Magdalen and the Apostles—a kind of performance which was not uncommon in the earlier ages of Christianity. I copy the Prose from the Roman Missal, in the prosaic form in which I have always seen it printed, and in which it is said in that service.

VICTIMÆ PASCHALI LAUDES.

Victimæ Paschali laudes immolent Christiani.

Agnus redemit oves: Christus innocens Patri reconciliavit peccatores.

Mors et vita duello conflixere mirando: dux vitæ mortuus, regnat vivus.

Dic nobis, Maria: quid vidisti in via?

Sepulcrum Christi viventis, et gloriam vidi resurgentis.

Angelicos testes, sudarium et vestes.

Surrexit Christus, spes mea: præcedet vos in Galilæam.

Scimus Christum surrexisse a mortuis vere. Tu nobis, victor, Rex, miserere.

TO THE PASCHAL VICTIM RAISE.

Christians, raise your grateful strain
To the Paschal victim, slain;
Now the Lamb the flock hath bought—
To the Father, long besought,
Christ, the pure and undefiled,
Hath the sinner reconciled.
Here contending Death and Life
Now have met in wondrous strife;
Death the Prince of Life hath slain,
Now he reigns in life again!
"Tell us, Mary, what, to-day,
Thou beheldest on thy way."
"Where the buried Lord had been,
There His glory I have seen,
Angel witnesses around,
Grave clothes that His body bound.
Christ, my hope, alive and free,
Follow Him to Galilee."
Christ, the just, for sinners slain,
From the dead is risen again.
Thee, our victor King, we know—
To us, now, Thy mercy show.

DE MYSTERIO ASCENSIONIS DOMINI.

Portas vestras æternales,
Triumphales, principales,
Angeli, attollite.
Eja, tollite actutum,
Venit Dominus virtutum,
Rex æternæ gloriæ.
Venit totus lætabundus,
Candidus et rubicundus,
Tinctis claris vestibus.
Nova gloriosus stola,
Gradiens virtute sola,
Multis cinctus millibus.
Solus erat in egressu,
Sed ingentem in regressu
Affert multitudinem,
Fructum suæ passionis,
Testem resurrectionis,
Novam cœli segetem,
Eja, jubilate Deo,
Jacent hostes, vicit Leo,
Vicit semen Abrahæ,
Jam ruinæ replebuntur,
Cœli cives augebuntur,
Salvabuntur animæ.

THE ASCENSION OF THE LORD.

Raise the everlasting gates,
Triumph now the Lord awaits—
Angels raise them hastily.
Open wide the pearly portal,
Now ascends the Lord immortal,
King of glory endlessly.
Now he comes in joy sufficing,
White and radiant in his rising—
Vestments dyed and glorious—
In new robes, to triumph rising,
Walking in his strength surprising,
With a throng victorious.
He, alone, to earth descended,
See him back to Heaven ascended,
Bringing thousands with him here—
Fruit of his incarnate dying—
To his rising testifying—
Heaven's harvest gathered here.
Shout aloud Jehovah's praises—
O'er his foes, the Lion raises
Triumph now to Abra'm's seed.
Now our ruin quickly ceases—
Now the heavenly host increases—
Souls will now be saved indeed

Regnet Christus triumphator
Hominumque liberator,
Rex misericordiæ,
Princeps pacis, Deus fortis
Vitæ dator, victor mortis,
Laus cœlestis curiæ.
Tu, qui cœlum reserasti.
Et in illo præparasti,
Locum tuis famulis,
Fac me tibi famulari,
Et te piis venerari
Hic in terra jubilis,
Ut post actum vitæ cursum,
Ego quoque scandens sursum
Te videre valeam,
Juxta Patrem considentem,
Triumphantem et regentem
Omnia per gloriam.

Christ shall make his reign enduring,
Man's redemption now securing,
  Pardoning with fidelity.
Heavenly hosts his praises singing,
He in strength and peace is bringing,
  Life and immortality.
Thou the gates of heaven unbarring,
Thou, within, a place preparing
  For thy servants dwelling here,
Let me with thy servants joining,
With thy worshippers combining,
  Praise thee while remaining here,
So that when my course is ended,
Rising as my Lord ascended,
  I may see thee ever there
With the Father—seated by Him—
Triumphing in glory nigh him—
  Reigning with him everywhere.

VENI, SANCTE SPIRITUS.

This hymn, which Trench declares to be the loveliest of all the hymns in the whole circle of Latin sacred poetry, is another of the four principal proses—the prose for Pentecost. Clichtoveus says that it is beyond all praise, as well on account of its remarkable grace and ease, as of the richness and fullness of its thoughts and the finished beauty of its construction, seeming to show that the author, "whoever he may have been," was filled by the Holy Spirit with a heavenly sweetness, which enabled him to pour forth such delightful thoughts in such comprehensive and appropriate language.

It has been attributed to various authors, among others to Pope Innocent III. and to Hermanus Contractus, a learned monk of St. Gall. It is now commonly attributed to Robert II., King of France. Archbishop Trench says there exists no sufficient reason for calling in question the attribution which has been commonly made of it to King Robert. I am very slow to doubt when so great an authority says there exists no sufficient reason for doubting, but I am compelled to say that I know of no sufficient proof that King Robert was really the author of it. I should be quite ready to believe that he had set it to music, if I were convinced that so beautiful a specimen of rhymed accented Latin verse had been written before his day. In the authority quoted on page 75, the prose written by him is said to be the *Sancti Spiritus adsit nobis gratia*, which is now usually attributed to Notker, the first writer of proses. I borrow from the "Seven great hymns" an extract from the Chronicle of St. Bertin: "Robert était tres pieux, prudent, lettré et suffisamment philosophe, mais surtout excellent musicien. Il composa la prose du St. Esprit, qui commence par ces mots, *Adsit nobis gratia*, les rhythmes *Judæ et Hierusalem*, et *Cornelius Centurio*, qu'il offrit à Rome sur l'autel de St. Pierre, noté avec le chant qui leur était propre, de même que l'antiphone *Eripe* et plusieurs autres beaux morceaux." The facts, that no mention is here made of this gem, and that Clichtoveus, a careful inquirer, who died in 1543, speaks of the authorship as unknown, or so much in dispute that he would not name the author, throw, certainly, some doubt on the question. I incline to the belief that this and the *Veni Creator* have lived by force of their innate vitality, and that, without any real evidence, they have been attributed to their illustrious supposed authors. Being worthy of the highest authorship, they would naturally enough be attributed to kings and popes.

VENI, SANCTE SPIRITUS.

Veni, sancte Spiritus,
Et emitte cœlitus
  Lucis tuæ radium.
Veni, Pater pauperum;
Veni, dator munerum;
  Veni, lumen cordium.
Consolator optime,
Dulcis hospes animæ,
  Dulce refrigerium.
In labore requies,
In æstu temperies,
  In fletu solatium.
O lux beatissima,
Reple cordis intima
  Tuorum fidelium.
Sine tuo numine
Nihil est in homine,
  Nihil est innoxium.
Lava quod est sordidum,
Riga quod est aridum,
  Sana quod est saucium.
Flecte quod est rigidum,
Fove quod est frigidum,
  Rege quod est devium.

COME, HOLY SPIRIT.

Holy Spirit from above,
Shine upon us in Thy love
  With Thy heavenly radiance.
Father of the poor below,
Who dost every gift bestow,
  Light our hearts to gladden us.
Of the soul the dearest guest,
Of the heart the sweetest rest,
  Sent of God to comfort us—
Freshness for the summer's heat,
In our tears a solace sweet,
  Sweet repose in weariness—
Let Thy faithful in Thy sight
Feel Thy cheering, heavenly light,
  Warming and enlightening us.
Oh! without Thy quickening power,
We must perish in an hour,
  Everything condemning us.
Wash away each guilty stain,
Water with Thy gracious rain,
  In Thy mercy healing us.
Move our stubborn lips to praise,
Warm our coldness with Thy rays,
  Call us from our wanderings.

Da tuis fidelibus
In te cofidentibus
  Sacrum septenarium.
Da virtutis meritum,
Da salutis exitum,
  Da perenne gaudium.

Them who on Thy grace depend,
Them, Thy faithful, ever send
  Sacred sevenfold peace with Thee.
Give them virtue's best reward,
Give salvation with the Lord;
  Give them joy unceasingly.

LAUDA, SION, SALVATOREM.

Of all the mediæval hymnologists, no one used the Latin rhymed versification in greater perfection than St. Thomas Aquinas, nor is there any hymn which better exhibits his remarkable power as a writer of Latin hymns, than the *Lauda Sion Salvatorem*, the prose for the holy sacrament, one of the four principal proses. As has been before stated (page 52), it, together with the *Pange, Lingua, Gloriosi*, was written by St. Thomas, as part of the office for the feast of the Holy Sacrament, composed by him, at the request of Pope Urban IV., when he instituted that divinely appointed rite as one of the regular festivals of the Roman Catholic Church.

According to his view of that solemn supper, he has in this prose exhausted the subject, not only in its theological and ecclesiastical sense, but in its administrative and receptive significance, while in the matter of versification it leaves nothing to be desired. Its harmony is without a jar, and the flow of its rhythm is as easy and undisturbed as aptly chosen words can make it, while its gentle cadences are in accord with the divine love which inspired the sacred rite. It is but just to say that he doubtless intended that his words should be understood according to the faith which the Roman Catholic Church now teaches; but it may also be said that the hymn might have been written by a Protestant, in the same words, without doing violence to the faith of the Protestant Church, although it does not fully express that faith; and I have preferred to translate it in that sense.

LAUDA, SION, SALVATOREM.

Lauda, Sion, Salvatorem,
Lauda ducem & pastorem
In hymnis & canticis.
Quantum potes, tantum aude,
Quia major omni laude,
Nec laudare sufficis.
Laudis thema specialis,
Panis vivus & vitalis
Hodie proponitur.
Quem in sacræ mensa cœnæ,
Turbæ fratrum duodenæ
Datum non ambigitur.
Sit laus plena, sit sonora:
Sit jucunda, sit decora
Mentis jubilatio.
Dies solemnis agitur,
In qua mensæ recolitur,
Hujus institutio.
In hac mensa novi Regis,
Novum Pascha novæ legis
Phase vetus terminat.
Vetustatem novitas,
Umbram fugat veritas,
Noctem lux eliminat.

SION, PRAISE THY SAVIOUR.

Sion, praise thine Interceder;
To thy Shepherd and thy Leader
  Songs and anthems elevate.
With thy highest powers sing Him,
Still the praises thou canst bring Him
  Never can be adequate.
Theme of praise, all praise transcending,
Bread of life, from heaven descending!
  He to us has offered it,
As He in that final meeting,
When the sacred twelve were eating.
  To them freely proffered it.
Lift aloud the voice of praising,
Sweet and holy accents raising,
  Strains divine to execute.
'Tis the solemn feast provided,
Where the Lord Himself presided,
  This His feast to institute.
Table of the Lord ascended,
Paschal Lamb for us intended,
  Ancient form here terminates.
New things now the old supplying,
From the truth the shadows flying,
  Light the darkness dissipates.

Quod in cœna Christus gessit,
Faciendum hoc expressit
In sui memoriam.
Docti sacris institutis,
Panem, vinum in salutis
Consecramus hostiam.
Dogma datur Christianis,
Quod in carnem transit panis,
Et vinum in sanguinem.
Quod non capis, quod non vides,
Animosa firmat fides,
Præter rerum ordinem.
Sub diversis speciebus,
Signis tantum & non rebus,
Latent res eximiæ.
Caro cibus, sanguis potus,
Manet tamen Christus totus
Sub utraque specie.
A sumente non concisus,
Non confractus, non divisus;
Integer accipitur.
Sumit unus, sumunt mille,
Quantum isti, tantum ille:
Nec sumptus consumitur.
Sumunt boni, sumunt mali,
Sorte tamen inæquali,
Vitæ vel interitus.
Mors est malis, vita bonis:
Vide paris sumptionis
Quam sit dispar exitus.

Doing what the Lord was doing,
Here, His own commandment showing,
We His love commemorate.
Taught by Jesus' inculcation,
Bread and wine for our salvation
Here to Him we dedicate.
Here to Christians Jesus preacheth,
Here to us the mystery teacheth,
Never sense perceiving it—
Flesh and blood, for us devoted,
Are by bread and wine denoted,
Living faith believing it.
In the different kinds He places,
Signs of hidden gifts and graces,
Precious things He telleth here:
That His flesh is meat unto us,
And His blood is drink unto us—
In them both He dwelleth here.
He this blessed bread that breaketh,
He that of this wine partaketh,
All the Saviour cherisheth;
All the Church on earth may break it,
All the faithful may partake it.
None of Jesus perisheth.
Good and bad, together meeting,
And the sacred supper eating,
Each how different taketh it!
To the wicked condemnation,
To the worthy sweet salvation,
Christ the Saviour maketh it!

Fracto demum Sacramento,
Ne vacilles, sed memento
Tantum esse sub fragmento
  Quantum toto tegitur.
Nulla rei fit scissura,
Signi tantum fit fractura,
Qua nec status nec statura
  Signati minuitur.
Ecce panis Angelorum,
Factus cibus viatorum:
Vere panis filiorum,
  Non mittendus canibus.
In figuris præsignatur,
Cum Isaac immolatur,
Agnus Paschæ deputatur,
  Datur manna patribus.
Bone Pastor, panis vere,
Jesu nostri miserere,
Tu nos pasce, nos tuere,
Tu nos bona fac videre
  In terra viventium.
Tu qui cuncta scis & vales,
Qui nos pascis hic mortales,
Tuos ibi commensales,
Cohæredes & sodales,
  Fac sanctorum civium.

When this sacred feast thou makest,
When thou but a morsel breakest,
Thou the Saviour still partakest—
He is all in all to thee.
By the sign that is divided,
Real food, for thee provided,
Still unbroke, to thee confided,
Jesus doth recall to thee.
Angel bread, from heaven descended,
Food to wanderers here extended,
For the children's bread intended,
Dogs should never take of it.
Isaac, as a type, promoted,
And the Paschal Lamb, devoted,
And the manna—all denoted
Only His might break of it.
Thou Good Shepherd, Bread of Heaven!
Jesus, let us be forgiven!
Feed and guard us by Thy kindness,
Take us from our earthly blindness
To the glory giv'n by Thee.
Thou, all powerful and all knowing—
Blessed food on us bestowing—
At Thy Table with Thee eating,
Thy coheirs together meeting,
Let us dwell in heaven with Thee!

ADAM OF ST. VICTOR.

The Abbey of St. Victor, near Paris, was one of the most celebrated religious houses in France seven hundred years ago—celebrated for its learning, its theology, its genuine devotion, and its fondness for sacred lyrics. It was, hence, the home and resort, as well as the parent and teacher, of great men. Among these Adam, a regular canon of the Abbey, was deservedly held in very high estimation for all the qualities of a devout and learned man. His familiarity with the Sacred Scriptures was most remarkable, and evidently could have been the result of nothing less than the most constant reading, and the most careful study and comparison, of the sacred writers in the riper years of his cultivated intellect. The Holy Word seemed to be almost the only language that he knew—so easily and gracefully did it flow from his pen in the harmonious lines of his lyrical compositions, of which one hundred and six are now extant. They all have the same general characteristics of style and versification, and in them all we are continually delighted with the felicity as well as the facility with which he writes, while he is sometimes brief and sententious without a parallel.

Trench, in his Sacred Latin Poetry, has given us many of the best of his lyrics, so many and so various that we are made familiar with his characteristics. We seem to know him. The only one of these which I have selected for this little book is his poem on the Martyrdom of St. Stephen, which Trench calls a sublime composition; and we see that it well deserves the name, when, in imagination, we take the place of the old monk and become a spectator of that first martyrdom, passing with him from the present to that early dawn of Christianity, and from the description of the bloody scene, to the rapt ecstasy in which he apostrophizes the suffering saint and beholds the sympathizing Saviour in the opening heaven, upholding him and strengthening him in the triumph of his martyrdom.

Dr. Trench accords to him the highest place among the writers of Latin Sacred Poetry, but not without some doubt whether that honor may not properly belong to Archbishop Hildebert. He would except the authors of the *Dies Iræ* and the *Stabat Mater*, if the harps on which those unequalled strains were improvised did not seem to have been immediately broken into silence.

He died July 8, 1177, and his epitaph, written by himself, was preserved for several hundred years on the walls of the Abbey, near the door of the choir, where the echo of his hymns had been so often heard. The tone of penitent humility, and the impressive, solemn, movement of the epitaph, have induced me to insert it here as a part of this sketch, to exhibit his character, by his own hand, as it was his last desire to appear.

EPITAPHIUM.

Hæres peccati, natura filius iræ,
Exiliique reus, nascitur omnis homo.
Unde superbit homo, cujus conceptio culpa,
Nasci pœna, labor vita, necesse mori?
Vana salus hominis, vanus decor, omnia vana—
Inter vana nihil vanius est homine—
Dum magis alludit præsentis gloria vitæ,
Præterit, immo fugit—non fugit, immo perit.
Post hominem vermis, post vermem fit cinis, heu, heu!
Sic redit ad cinerem gloria nostra simul.
Hic ego qui jaceo, miser et miserabilis Adam,
Unam pro summo munere posco precem—
Peccavi, fateor, veniam peto, parce fatenti,
Parce pater; fratres parcite; parce Deus!

EPITAPH.

An heir of sin and child of wrath by nature here
below,
A stranger every man is born—an exile's life to
know.
Whence doth he boast himself in pride whose
thought is guilt, innate,
Whose birth is pain, whose life is toil, and death
his only fate?
Vain health of man, vain beauty too, vain boast of
earthly pride,
Vain thing is man, among the vain, vainer than all
beside.
The glory of this present life, what time it doth
delight,
Doth quickly pass, not pass but fly, not fly but
perish quite.
And then, to man the worm succeeds, and after
worms the dust,
At once to dust he must return with every earthly
trust.
And I, poor Adam lying here, 'tis mercy all I need,
One only prayer I now can make—for heaven's
last gift I plead,
My sins confess, my pardon seek—oh let a sinner live!
Father, and brothers in the faith, and God, oh God,
forgive!

DE. S. STEPHANO.

Heri mundus exultavit,
Et exultans celebravit
Christi natalitia.
Heri chorus angelorum
Prosecutus est cœlorum
Regem cum lætitia.
Protomartyr et Levita,
Clarus fide, clarus vita,
Clarus et miraculis,
Sub hac luce triumphavit,
Et triumphans insultavit
Stephanus incredulis.
Fremunt ergo tanquam feræ,
Quia victi defecere
Lucis adversarii.
Falsos testes statuunt,
Et linguas exacuunt
Viperarum filii.
Agonista, nulli cede—
Certa certus de mercede,
Persevera Stephane—
Insta falsis testibus,
Confuta sermonibus
Synagogam Satanæ.

ST. STEPHEN.

Yesterday the world, elated,
With their praises celebrated
  Jesus Christ's nativity;
Angels, then their voices raising,
Were the King of Heaven praising,
  Joyful in festivity.
Stephen, proto-martyr, Deacon,
In his faith and life a beacon,
  Mighty, too, in miracles,
This day, to his triumph rising,
Was in triumph then despising
  Cruel Jews and infidels.
They like beasts of prey were raging,
Their secure defeat presaging,
  And of light the enemies—
Lying witnesses providing,
And with sharpened tongues deriding—
  Sons of vipers venomous!
Stephen, strive, thy strife enduring,
And thy sure reward securing,
  Persevere to victory.
Fear not witnesses abounding,
All confute, with truth confounding
  Satan's desperate synagogue.

Fortis tuus est in cœlis,
Testis verax et fidelis,
Testis innocentiæ.
Nomen habes coronati,
Te tormenta decet pati
Pro corona gloriæ.
Pro corona non marcenti
Perfer brevis vim tormenti,
Te manet victoria.
Tibi fiet mors, natalis,
Tibi pœna terminalis
Dat vitæ primordia.
En! a dextris Dei stantem
Jesum, pro te dimicantem,
Stephane, considera.
Tibi cœlos reserari,
Tibi Christum revelari
Clama voce libera.
Plenus sancto spiritu
Penetrat intuitu
Stephanus cœlestia.
Videns Dei gloriam
Crescit ad victoriam,
Suspirat ad præmia.
Se commendat Salvatori,
Pro quo dulce ducit mori
Sub ipsis lapidibus.
Saulus servat omnium
Vestes lapidantium,
Lapidans in omnibus.

In the skies thy witness liveth,
And, in faith and truth, he giveth
Fullest proof of innocence.
Crownéd is the name thou wearest,
And the tortures that thou bearest
Give thy crown its radiance.
For a crown of light, unfading,
Meet the force of pain, invading—
Victory shall remain with thee.
Death to thee becometh natal,
For its final pang so fatal,
Giveth endless life to thee.
See, by God's right hand is standing
Jesus, for thee help commanding—
Stephen, see he aideth thee;
For thee, heavenly gates unsealing,
For thee, Christ the Lord revealing—
Cry unto him earnestly.
Stephen is to heaven gazing,
On the heavenly scenes amazing—
Holy Ghost sustaining him;
God's full glory to him showing,
While to victory he is going—
Love and hope constraining him.
To the Lord his soul commending,
Sweet he finds the death impending,
While the stones are bruising him;
And young Saul, the garments holding
Of those stoning, is upholding,
And, himself, is using them.

Ne peccatum statuatur
His, a quibus lapidatur
Genu ponit et precatur,
Condolens insaniæ—
In Christo sic obdormivit,
Qui Christo sic obedivit,
Et cum Christo semper vivit,
Martyrum primitiæ.

"Lord forgive them," hear him saying,
For the men who him are slaying,
On his bended knee now praying—
  Praying God to pardon them.
Thus, in Christ, the martyr sleeping,
To him thus obedience keeping,
In him liveth without weeping—
  First fruits these of martyrdom.

DIES IRÆ.

"Of all the Latin hymns of the Church, this has the widest fame. The grand use which Goethe has made of it in his *Faust* may have helped to bring it to the knowledge of some who would not otherwise have known it, or, if they had, would not have believed its worth, if the sage and seer of this world, a prophet of their own, had not thus set his seal of recognition upon it. To another illustrious man this hymn was eminently dear. How affecting is that incident recorded of Sir Walter Scott by his biographer, how, in those last days of his, when all of his great mind had failed, or was failing, he was yet heard to murmur to himself some lines of this hymn, an especial favorite with him in other days. Nor is it hard to account for its wide and general popularity. The metre, so grandly devised, of which I remember no other example, fitted though it has here shown itself for bringing out some of the noblest powers of the Latin language; the solemn effort of the triple rhyme, which has been likened to blow following blow of the hammer on the anvil; the confidence of the poet in the universal interest of his theme, a confidence which has made him set out his matter with so majestic and unadorned a plainness as at once to be intelligible to all—these merits, with many more, have given the *Dies Iræ* a foremost place among the master-pieces of sacred song."—TRENCH.

Its great power, its universal sympathy with every man, lies in its absolute selfishness—not in a bad sense, in the highest and purest and best sense—and in the sincerity and earnestness of its simple and natural language. It is the language of one man, in relation to himself alone, in view of the awful realities of that ultimate responsibility which all right-minded men so often feel, and which all men, the most hardened even, sometimes feel with great solemnity. The conflagration, the judge, the trumpet, the book, the whole scene, are mentioned only to give force to the exclamation, "*Quid sum, miser! tunc dicturus?*" "What can I then say?" And every confession and every prayer is for individual self, and is a renunciation of all hope, except through the free grace of Christ. The last stanza is omitted in some copies. Trench omits it, as do some others. If it be translated, as it sometimes is, as a prayer for the salvation of all mankind at the last day, then it certainly is not in harmony with the rest of the hymn, and ought to be omitted. On the other hand, if it be translated as it is here, and has been by some others, and as it clearly should be, rendering the last line "Spare me," then the last stanza, instead of being feeble and inconsequent, becomes a harmonious and proper close of a hymn with such a beginning.

It is usually ascribed to Thomas of Celano, an Italian monk of the thirteenth century; but I think, with Trench, that there is no certainty—I should say but little probability—that the authorship belongs to him.

DIES IRÆ.

Dies iræ, dies illa!
Solvet sæclum in favilla,
Teste David cum Sybilla.
Quantus tremor est futurus,
Quando Judex est venturus,
Cuncta stricte discussurus.
Tuba mirum spargens sonum
Per sepulcra regionum,
Coget omnes ante thronum.
Mors stupebit, et natura,
Quum resurget creatura,
Judicanti responsura.
Liber scriptus proferetur,
In quo totum continetur,
Unde mundus judicetur.
Judex ergo cum sedebit,
Quidquid latet, apparebit:
Nil inultum remanebit.
Quid sum, miser! tunc dicturus
Quem patronum rogaturus,
Quum vix justus sit securus?

THE DAY OF WRATH.

Day of threatened wrath from heaven,
To the sinful, unforgiven!
Earth on fire, to ashes driven!
Oh, the guilty, how affrighted!
That each wrong shall then be righted,
And with blazing truth be lighted!
Loud the trumpet will be blowing,
All on earth the sound be knowing,
And to answer will be going.
Death amazed will then be quaking—
As the dead of ages waking,
Shall their fearful doom be taking.
From the Book then opened newly,
Every sinful deed must, duly,
Then be heard and answered truly.
God, the Judge, will then be dealing,
With each hidden thought and feeling,
And the last award be sealing.
What shall wretched I be saying?
To what Friend for help be praying?
Fear the righteous then dismaying!

Rex tremendæ majestatis,
Qui salvandos salvas gratis,
Salva me, fons pietatis!
Recordare, Jesu pie,
Quod sum causa tuæ viæ;
Ne me perdas illa die!
Quærens me, sedisti lassus,
Redemisti, crucem passus:
Tantus labor non sit cassus.
Juste Judex ultionis,
Donum fac remissionis
Ante diem rationis.
Ingemisco tanquam reus,
Culpa rubet vultus meus;
Supplicanti parce, Deus!
Qui Mariam absolvisti,
Et latronem exaudisti,
Mihi quoque spem dedisti.
Preces meæ non sunt dignæ,
Sed Tu bonus fac benigne
Ne perenni cremer igne!
Inter oves locum præsta,
Et ab hædis me sequestra,
Statuens in parte dextra.
Confutatis maledictis,
Flammis acribus addictis,
Voca me cum benedictis!
Oro supplex et acclinis,
Cor contritum quasi cinis,
Gere curam mei finis.

King of Kings, all powers enthralling,
Without price Thy chosen calling,
Pity, save my soul from falling!
Jesus, cradled in a manger—
For my sake on earth a stranger—
Save me in that day of danger!
For me weary, all things needing—
On the cross in anguish bleeding—
Do not lose such toil and pleading!
God the righteous, never sleeping!
Oh! forgive a sinner weeping!
While Thy love is mercy keeping!
Lost without Thy blood atoning—
Blushes mingling with my groaning—
Spare my soul in sorrow moaning!
Sinful Mary Thou forgavest,
And the dying thief Thou savedst,
Ground of hope to me Thou gavest.
Prayers unworthy to Thee sending,
Be Thy goodness still befriending;
Save me from the fire unending!
With Thy chosen flock forever,
When the sheep and goats shall sever
On Thy right hand keep me ever!
When, in fire, the cursèd gather,
Let me hear Thee saying, rather,
"Come, thou blessed of my Father!"
Trusting to Thy goodness wholly—
Crushed in heart, and bending lowly—
Save at last, Thou Just and Holy!

Lacrymosa dies illa!
Qua resurget ex favilla,
Judicandus homo reus;
Huic ergo parce, Deus!

In that day when, weeping, quaking,
Man shall rise, from dust awaking,
In thine arms, O Jesus! bear me—
From Thy curses, God, oh! spare me!

THE DAY OF WRATH.

ANOTHER VERSION.

Day of wrath! that final day,
Shall the world in ashes lay!
David and the Sibyl say.
Oh! what trembling there shall be,
When the coming Judge we see,
All to try impartially!
When the trumpet's awful sound
Bursts the graves beneath the ground,
Calling all the throne around.
Death amazed, and Nature, too,
See the dead arise to view,
To their just and final due.
There the record will be shown,
In which everything is known,
Whence to judge the world alone.
When the Judge is seated, then
Shall each sin appear again—
Not unpunished one remain.
Wretched me! what shall I say?
Who will plead for me that day,
When the just themselves must pray?

King of Majesty divine!
Freely saving who are Thine,
Save me, Fount of Love divine!
Blessed Jesus! think, I pray,
For me was Thy weary way—
Do not lose me in that day!
Sought by Thee in toil and pain,
By Thy cross redeemed again,
Let Thy sufferings not be vain!
Judge! Thy vengeance, oh! delay;
Grant me pardon, here I pray,
Now, before that reckoning day.
Humbly I my sorrow speak,
Blushes burn my guilty cheek,
Spare me, God, while thus I seek;
Mary, Thy free grace forgave,
Grace the dying thief did save,
Hope of grace to me it gave.
All unworthy is my prayer,
But thy goodness still declare;
Let me not in flames despair!
When Thy sheep, by Thy command,
From the goats divided stand,
Place me then on Thy right hand.
When the cursèd in their shame
Writhe in everlasting flame,
With the blessed call my name.
Bowed and lowly, hear my cry!
See my heart in ashes lie!
Oh! protect me when I die!

On that final day of tears,
When before Thy bar appears
Man, from ashes risen again,
Spare me, God, oh! spare me then!

THE DAY OF WRATH.

ANOTHER VERSION.

Day of wrath, with vengeance glowing,
Seer and Sybil long foreknowing!
Earth and time to ruin going!
How the guilty world will tremble
When the Judge shall all assemble,
And not one will dare dissemble!
When the trumpet's summons, swelling
Through Death's dark and dusty dwelling,
To the throne is all compelling!
Death with fear will then be quailing,
As the dead of ages, wailing,
Rise to judgment, without failing.
Then the book of God's own writing—
Truth alone the pages lighting—
Will be guilty souls indicting,
Every secret thought and feeling,
To the Judge at once revealing,
None excusing, none concealing.

How shall wretched I be pleading?
Through what patron interceding,
When the just are mercy needing?
King, all majesty expressing,
By free grace, Thy saved possessing,
Save me, Fount of heavenly blessing!
Jesus, think what woes thou tasted,
While for me to death thou hasted;
Let them not at last be wasted.
Thou didst seek me, sad and sighing,
God forsaken in Thy dying!
Be not fruitless all Thy trying.
Righteous Judge, thy wrath delaying,
Pardon me while I am praying!
While the day of grace is staying.
Groaning, guilty, hear me speaking!
Blushes, sin and shame bespeaking;
Spare me, Lord, thy pardon seeking.
Sinful Mary was forgiven,
Thou didst call the thief to heaven,
Hope to me was also given.
Worthless are the prayers I'm raising;
Save me by Thy grace, amazing,
From the fire for ever blazing!
From the goats, O Lord, divide me!
And among Thy sheep, beside Thee,
On Thy right, my place provide me.
When the cursèd, downward driven,
To eternal flames are given,
Call me with the blest to heaven.

Listen, Lord, to my petition—
Crushed in heart, in deep contrition—
Save, oh! save me, from perdition.
On that day of bitter weeping,
When from dust and mortal sleeping,
Man is called to final hearing,
Spare me, God, on my appearing!

THOMAS À KEMPIS.

Thomas à Kempis—Thomas Hamerken of Campen or Kempen—was born at Kempen in the Province of Over Yssel in Holland in 1380. He was educated at the University of Deventer, the Capital of the province, and afterwards entered among members of the Monastery of Mount St. Agnes, of the Order of St. Augustin. He there displayed great piety, patience and self-denial. He joined the Order of the Brothers of the Common Life, which was first established at Deventer, by Gerhard, the great, who was a native of Over Yssel. The members of that order had no monastic vows and devoted their lives to preaching and to teaching letters and religion to the young, supporting themselves by their industry, which they applied, principally, to copying books. He died in 1471, in the 91st year of his age.

Wherever the Gospel is preached, the influence of this devout man is felt. The "Imitation of Christ," which is now generally attributed to him, next after the Bible has been more frequently printed and more widely read, than any other religious book. It has been translated into every Christian language, and has been the welcome companion of devout Christians of every denomination. It is said that a traveling monk found an Arabic copy of it in the library of a king of Morocco, which his Moorish majesty prized beyond all his other books.

The following is considered the best of his poems.

DE GAUDIIS CŒLESTIBUS.

Astant angelorum chori,
Laudes cantant Creatori,
Regem cernunt in decore,
Amant corde, laudant ore.
Tympanizant, citharizant,
Volant alis, stant in scalis,
Sonant nolis, fulgent stolis.
Coram Summa Trinitate,
Clamant Sanctus, Sanctus, Sanctus!
  Fugit dolor, cessat planctus
In superna civitatę.
Concors vox est omnium,
Deum collaudentium.
Fervet amor mentium
Clare contuentium,
Beatam Trinitatem in una Deitate,
Quam adorant Seraphim
Ferventi in amore,
Venerantur Cherubim
Ingenti sub honore—
Mirantur nimis Throni de tanta majes-
tate.

THE JOYS OF HEAVEN.

Angel choirs on high are singing,
To the Lord their praises bringing,
Yielding him in royal beauty
Heart and voice, in love and duty;
Waving wings the throne surrounding,
Timbrels, harps, and bells are sounding,
See their heavenly vestments glisten,
To their heavenly music listen;
Hear them, by the Godhead staying,
Holy, holy, holy, saying.
None that grieveth, or complaineth,
In that heavenly land remaineth—
Every voice, in concord joining
Holy praise to God combining.
Holy love their minds disposeth,
Heavenly light to all discloseth
Blessed Three in God united—
Seraphs worshipping delighted,
Sweet affection overflowing—
Cherubim their rev'rence showing,
Bowing low, their pinions folding—
God's majestic throne beholding.

Oh quam preclara regio!
Et quam decora legio
Ex angelis et hominibus!
Oh gloriosa civitas,
In qua summa tranquillitas,
Lux et pax in cunctis finibus!
Cives hujus civitatis
Veste nitent castitatis,
Legem tenent caritatis,
Firmum pactum unitatis.
Non laborant, nil ignorant.
Non tentantur, nec vexantur,
Semper sani, semper læti,
Cunctis bonis sunt repleti.

Oh! what fair and heavenly region!
Oh! what bright and glorious legion,
Saints and angels, all excelling!
In that glorious city dwelling,
Which in rest divine reposeth,
And sweet light and peace discloseth!
Every one who there resideth,
Clad in purity abideth,
Charity their spirits joining—
Firm in unity combining—
Toil nor ign'rance undergoing—
Trouble nor temptation knowing:
Always health and joy undying,
To them every good supplying.

THE DAY OF DEATH.

·DAMIANI.

St. Peter Damiani was an illustrious Doctor of the Catholic Church in the eleventh century. He was born at Ravenna, about the year 1006, and he died at Faenza, in 1072. He is said to have been a swine-herd in his youth, and to have been taken from that humble employment by his brother, who was Archdeacon of Ravenna, and educated under his care. On the completion of his studies he quit the world and entered the Hermitage of Font-Avellana, and in 1061 was made Abbot of it. He was so much impressed with the crimes and vices of the age in which he lived, many of which had entered the Church, that he devoted his energies to their reformation, especially so far as the clergy were concerned, and with the greatest zeal coöperated with the popes of his time, Gregory VI., Clement II., Leo IX., Victor II., and Stephen IX., in their efforts to reform the Church. Stephen created him Cardinal Bishop of Ostia. The ostentation of that office, however, ill-befitted his love of solitude and devotion, and he resigned his hat and returned to the Hermitage as a simple monk, ten years before he died. He was several times called out of it to perform missions of great importance, but in the midst of courts, as well as in the Hermitage, he lived in poverty and austerity.

The following hymn, *De Die Mortis*, is among the best of his many poems. I take it from Trench. I do not know whether it has been before translated. I have selected it for its solemn movement, its descriptive details, its striking images, its devout aspirations, and its impressive doctrine—all in harmony with the subject.

In a note to this devout hymn of Damiani, Trench copies at length the hymn of the *Cygnus Exspirans*, which I have inserted here for its striking contrast with the *De Die Mortis*, and for its beauty as well. It is found in some modern collections of mediæval hymns, without the name, so far as I know, of even a supposed author, and it seems to lack the marks as well as the unction of mediæval song—hardly hinting at religion. With the exception of one or two stanzas, it might, so far as Christianity is concerned, have been written by Epicurus. Trench says of it: "I know no fitter place to append a poem which can claim no room in the body of this collection, being almost without any distinctly Christian element whatever, and little more than a mere worldly lamentation at leaving a world which he knows he has abused, yet would willingly, if he might, continue still longer to abuse. But even from that, something may be learned, and there is a force and originality about the composition which make me willing to insert it here, especially as it is very far from common. I would gladly know something more about it." The title found in the books is retained here, although I once caused it to be published under the title of The Dying Voluptuary.

DE DIE MORTIS.

Gravi me terrore pulsas, vitæ dies ultima;
Moeret cor, solvuntur renes, læsa tremunt viscera,
Tuam speciem dum sibi mens depingit anxia.

Quis enim pavendum illud explicet spectaculum,
Quum, dimenso vitæ cursu, carnis ægra nexibus
Anima luctatur solvi, propinquans ad exitum?

Perit sensus, lingua riget, resolvuntur oculi,
Pectus palpitat, anhelat raucum guttur hominis,
Stupent membra, pallent ora, decor abit corporis.

Præsto sunt et cogitatus, verba, cursus, opera,
Et præ oculis nolentis glomerantur omnia:

THE DAY OF DEATH.

With terror thou dost strike me now, life's fearful dying day—
My heart is sad, my loins are weak, my spirit faints away,
While to my saddened soul, thy sight my anxious thoughts display.

Who can that dreadful sight describe, or without trembling see,
When from the ended course of life, the weary soul would flee,
And, sick of all the bonds of flesh, it struggles to be free?

The senses fail, the tongue is stiff, the eyes uncertain stray—
The panting breath and gasping throat, the coming end betray—
From palsied limbs and pallid lips all charm has fled away.

Now spring at once to view, past thoughts and words and deeds and life—
Before unwilling eyes they come, all crowding fresh and rife,

Illuc tendat, huc se vertat, coram videt
posita.
Torquet ipsa reum sinum mordax con-
scientia,
Plorat apta corrigendi defluxisse tempora;
Plena luctu caret fructu sera pœniten-
tia.
Falsa tunc dulcedo carnis in amarum
vertitur,
Quando brevem voluptatem perpes pœna
sequitur;
Jam quod magnum credebatur nil fuisse
cernitur.
Quæso, Christe, rex invicte, tu succurre
misero,
Sub extrema mortis hora cum jussus
abiero,
Nullum in me jus tyranno præbeatur
impio.
Cadat princeps tenebrarum, cadat pars
tartarea;
Pastor, ovem jam redemptam tunc reduc
ad patriam,
Ubi te videndi causa perfruar in sæcula.

And stand revealed before the mind, that shrinks with timid strife.
And biting conscience tortures now the trembling, guilty, breast,
And weeps the loss of perished hours, that might have given rest—
Too late repentance, full of grief, no proper fruit has blessed.
Of the false sweetness of the flesh, what bitterness remains,
When the brief pleasure of this life, is turned to endless pains,
And all life's idols here below, the dying hour disdains.
I pray Thee, Jesus, grant me, then, Thine own almighty aid,
When I shall enter at the last, in death's dark valley shade—
Let not the tyrant foe, I pray, my trembling soul invade.
O! from the Prince of Darkness, then, and hell's dark prison save!
And take me ransomed to Thy home, Good Shepherd, now I crave,
Where I may live in endless life, with Thee beyond the grave.

CYGNUS EXSPIRANS.

Parendum est, cedendum est,
Claudenda vitæ scena;
Est jacta sors, me vocat mors,
Hæc hora est postrema:
Valete res, valete spes;
Sic finit cantilena.
O magna lux, sol, mundi dux,
Est concedendum fatis;
Duc lineam eclipticam,
Mihi luxisti satis:
Nox incubat; fax occidit;
Jam portum subit ratis.
Tu Cynthia argentea,
Vos, aurei planetæ,
Cum stellulis, ocellulis,
Nepotibus lucete;
Fatalia, letalia
Mi nunciant cometæ.
Ter centies, ter millies
Vale, immunde munde!
Instabilis et labilis,
Vale, orbis rotunde!

THE DYING SWAN.

I must obey, I may not stay,
The scene of life is ending,
The lot is cast, Death calls at last,
My final hour's impending.
Farewell estate and hopes elate—
All like a song are ending.
Thou glorious sun, my day is done,
But thou, thy journey keeping,
Go on thy way, great king of day—
I must in death be sleeping.
Night's pall is spread, the light is fled,
My bark to port is sweeping.
Thou moon serene with silver sheen,
Ye planets golden seeming,
And little eyes that star the skies,
For my descendants beaming,
The Fates' decree of death to me,
Is told by comets streaming.
Three hundred times, three thousand times
Farewell, thou world defiling,
Unsteady thou and slippery now,
Farewell, with all thy smiling.

Mendaciis, fallaciis,
Lusisti me abunde.
  Lucentia, fulgentia
Gemmis valete tecta,
Seu marmore, seu ebore
Supra nubes erecta.
Ad parvulum me loculum
Mors urget equis vecta.
  Lucretiæ, quæ specie
Gypsata me cepistis,
Imagines, voragines!
Quæ mentem sorbuistis,
En oculos, heu! scopulos,
Extinguit umbra tristis.
  Tripudia, diludia,
Et fescennini chori,
Quiescite, raucescite;
Præco divini fori,
Mors, intonat et insonat
Hunc lessum; Debes mori.
  Deliciæ, lautitiæ
Mensarum cum culina;
Cellaria, bellaria,
Et coronata vina,
Vos nauseo, dum haurio
Quem scyphum mors propinat.
  Facessite, putrescite,
Odores, vestimenta;
Rigescite, deliciæ,

With falsehoods sweet and artful cheat
No longer me beguiling.
  Ye castles bright, with gems bedight,
Farewell! in air erected,
With marble walls or ivory halls,
In Fancy's skies reflected.
I seek my bed among the dead,
By Death's pale steeds directed.
  Ye beauties rare, whose charms so fair,
My captive sense delighted;
Delirious dream of love supreme
That all my mind excited,
Your siren eyes, where danger lies,
Are now in death benighted.
  Ye dances vain and sports profane,
In wanton chorus singing,
Be still I pray, your orgies stay,
God's summons now is ringing—
His crier, Death, with startling breath
My mortal sentence bringing.
  Delights of life with luxury rife,
The table's social pleasure;
The dainty meats, the honeyed sweets,
And wine-cup's crownéd treasure.
I loathe you all, while Death doth call
To pledge his brimming measure.
  Haste ye away, fade and decay,
Ye rich perfumes and dresses;
Be cold and stale, ye pleasures frail,

Libidinum fomenta!
Deformium me vermium
Manent operimenta.
  O culmina, heu! fulmina,
Horum fugax honorum,
Tam subito dum subeo
Æternitatis domum.
Ridiculi sunt tituli;
Foris et agunt momum.
  Lectissimi, carissimi
Amici et sodales,
Heu! insolens et impudens
Mors interturbat sales.
Sat lusibus indulsimus:
Extremum dico vale!
  Tu denique, corpus, vale,
Te, te citabit forum;
Te conscium, te socium
Dolorum et gaudiorum!
Æqualis nos expectat sors—
Bonorum vel malorum.

Provoking love's caresses.
Foul worms shall dress, in loathsomeness,
The grave my body presses.
  On glory's height, what bolts may light!
I leave these honors fleeting;
As hence I go, my fate to know,
Eternity now meeting.
Title and fame and noble name,
How worthless and how cheating!
  Ye chosen few, my comrades true,
Dear friends my pleasure sharing;
Insulting Death stops every breath,
No wit or wisdom sparing:
And here to-day I leave our play,
My last farewell declaring.
  Body, farewell! thy fate I tell,
This final summons hearing;
Thou too hast known and called thine own,
My griefs and joys endearing.
Body and mind, in life combined,
One goal are always nearing.

PRUDENTIUS.

Aurelius Clemens Prudentius was a native of Spain, born in the year 348. He was bred a lawyer, and although his youth was stained with follies and vices upon which, in later life, he looked back with shame and disgust, and his professional career was less characterized by a love of justice than an unscrupulous strife for success, he filled many high civil and military stations under the Emperors Theodosius, and his sons, Arcadius and Honorius, including eminent judicial positions, in which he says:

> Bis legum moderamine
> Frenos nobilium reximus urbium,
> Jus civile bonis redidimus, terruimus reos.

He finally withdrew from the honors and employments of the world, to the quiet of a religious and literary life. He wrote many poems of great but unequal merit, all of them exhibiting the characteristic culture of a man of the world, whose philosophic mind, trained in the schools and versed in the sharpening activities of earnest professional and public life, had voluntarily left those profane honors and enjoyments for the purer tastes and higher pleasures of humility and devotion. His *Cathemerinon* is considered the best of his works. It consists of a collection of poems appropriate to the duties of daily life. "*Hymni omnibus diurnis actionibus convenientes.*" His funeral hymn, *Hymnus in Exequiis Defunctorum* is the tenth of these, and is by common consent the best of all his hymns. It is a noble poem on Death, the Grave, and the Resurrection, consisting of forty-three stanzas, portions of which, sometimes more and sometimes less, selected variously, have been published in collections, Protestant as well as Catholic. I have not seen anywhere, except in Trench, the concluding portion of the hymn separated from all the rest. In the following hymn I have taken the same concluding stanzas, considering them to have, besides their individual beauty, a collective unity and beauty which have not always been found in the other selections, and which commend them, especially, to quiet, religious contemplation.

The time of the death of Prudentius, as well as the place of his birth, are unknown.

IN EXEQUIIS DEFUNCTORUM.

Jam moesta quiesce querela,
Lachrymas suspendite, matres,
Nullus sua pignora plangat,
Mors haec reparatio vitæ est.
Sic semina sicca virescunt,
Jam mortua jamque sepulta,
Quæ reddita cæspite ab imo
Veteres meditantur aristas.
Nunc suscipe, terra, fovendum,
Gremioque hunc concipe molli,
Hominis tibi membra sequestro,
Generosa et fragmina credo.
Animæ fuit haec domus olim,
Factoris ab ore creatæ,
Fervens habitavit in istis
Sapientia principe Christo.
Tu depositum tege corpus,
Non immemor ille requiret
Sua munera fictor et auctor,
Propriique ænigmata vultus.
Veniant modo tempora justa,
Cum spem Deus impleat omnem,
Reddas patefacta necesse est,
Qualem tibi trado figuram.

A FUNERAL HYMN.

Be still the voice of sorrow here—
Ye mothers, dry your weeping eyes—
Let no one mourn his children dear—
From death a better life shall rise.
Dry seeds begin to live anew,
When dead and buried in the ground—
And from the earth restored to view,
In living blades again are found.
This body take to cherish, Earth,
As to thy gentle bosom's dust,
These limbs, to which thou gavest birth,
These noble relics we entrust.
For here once dwelt a living soul,
Created by the breath divine—
And wisdom, Jesus did control,
These mortal relics did enshrine.
Protect thou, Earth, the body, then,
Within the grave in silence laid,
For God will call to Him again,
What was in His own image made.
The time shall surely come once more,
When hope shall see these relics live—
When thou must open and restore
The form which now to thee we give.

Non si cariosa vetustas
Dissolverit ossa favillis,
Fueritque ciniscuIus arens
Minimi mensura pugilli:
Nec si vaga flumina, et auræ,
Vacuum per inane volantes,
Tulerint cum pulvere nervos,
Hominem periisse licebit.
Sed dum resolubile corpus
Revocas, Deus, atque reformas,
Quanam regione jubebis
Animam requiescere puram?
Gremio senis abdita sancti
Recubabit, ut illa Lazari,
Quem floribus undique septum
Dives procul aspicit ardens.
Sequimur tua dicta, Redemptor,
Quibus atra a morte triumphans,
Tua per vestigia mandas
Socium crucis ire latronem.
Patet ecce fidelibus ampli
Via lucida jam paradisi,
Licet et nemus illud adire,
Homini quod ademerat anguis.
Nos tecta fovebimus ossa
Violis et fronde frequenti,
Titulumque et frigida saxa
Liquido spargemus odore.

Nor if the perishing decay
Should turn these bones to ashes here,
And but the smallest handful stay
To show where now these limbs appear—
Nor should the winds and waters rise,
And hence in sweeping currents bear
This frame and earth wherein it lies,
Could man be made to perish there.
But when the changed and mouldered frame,
Thou, God, shalt call and form anew,
Where is the place Thou wilt proclaim
Home of the spirit pure and true?
'Twill lie in Abraham's bosom blest,
As that of Lazarus did of old,
Whom, wrapt in flowers of heavenly rest,
Dives in torment did behold.
Thy words, Redeemer, are our guide,
In dying triumph said by Thee,
When to the thief who with Thee died,
Thou saidst he should Thy glory see.
And thus the faithful may behold
The shining path to Paradise,
And walk that garden grove, of old,
The Serpent took from human eyes.
Here we will deck these buried bones
With violets and garlands fair,
And on their monumental stones
Will sprinkle odors fresh and rare.

www.ingramcontent.com/pod-product-compliance
Lightning Source LLC
LaVergne TN
LVHW021404110826
845150LV00007B/1776

* 9 7 8 1 4 2 5 5 1 2 3 5 4 *